Pioneers of the Street Railway in the USA,
Street Tramways in the UK ... and elsewhere

OTHER WORKS BY JOHN R. STEVENS:

An Account of the Construction and Embellishment of Old Time Ships, (1949)
Early History of Street Railways: The New Haven Area, (1982)
The Derby Horse Railway and the World's First Electric Freight Locomotive, (1987)
Pioneers of the Electric Railroad, (1991)
Dutch Vernacular Architecture in North America, 1640–1830, (2005)

OTHER WORKS BY ALAN W. BROTCHIE (*inter alia*):

Tramways of the Tay Valley, (1965)
Scottish Tramway Fleets, (1968)
Tramways of Fife and the Forth Valley, (Five volumes, 1975–8)
Fife's Trams and Buses, (1990)
Stirling's Trams and Buses, (1991)
Lanarkshire's Trams and Buses, (1993)
The Wemyss Private Railway, (1998)
Falkirk's Trams and Early Buses, (2011)
Rothesay's Trams and Buses, (2014)

With Harry Jack:
Early Railways of West Fife, (2007)

Pioneers of the Street Railway in the USA, Street Tramways in the UK ... and elsewhere

John R. Stevens and Alan W. Brotchie

To Finn —
John R. Stevens,
& Nov 29, 2016

Stenlake Publishing Ltd

First published in 2014 by
Stenlake Publishing Ltd
54–58 Mill Square
Catrine, Ayrshire
Scotland
KA5 6RD
Telephone: 01290 551122
www.stenlake.co.uk

ISBN: 978 1 84033 363 3

The publisher regret that they cannot supply
copies of any pictures featured in this book.

British Library Cataloguing-in-Publication Data
A catalogue record for this book is available
from the British Library

Designed by Mark Blackadder

Printed by ColorPage in Kingston, NY-USA

Contents

Introduction

This work was conceived by John Stevens to commemorate the one hundred and fifty year anniversary of the inauguration of the opening of the first street railway – or 'tramway' – in the United Kingdom at Birkenhead on 30 August 1860. His intention was (and is) to record how and why this came about, and place on record the achievements of the various pioneers in the field. That anniversary has come and gone, but the purpose of this work remains as was his original intention. Unfortunately execution has taken longer than intended.

While he worked on the American side of the story John looked for assistance in completing the story of George Francis Train in England.

After several false starts I was approached and agreed to attempt to add a chapter on events on this side of the 'pond'. As my interest developed I soon realised that much of what had been written regarding the earliest street railway days in England was severely biased (sometimes completely erroneous) and dependent on the autobiography dictated by Train in his 74th year – and which was soon proved to be exceedingly selective (or at fault) and I felt that to do the subject justice more than just a further reiteration of previously published work was necessary. As the story unfolded, by intensive use of on-line resources accessible now which have not been available to earlier writers, an entirely different picture has emerged. Because of the sometimes controversial nature of some events recorded, I have considered it vital to give the provenance of the contemporary sources.

No attempt has been made to merge the two halves of the story. John has written with American usage, I have written with British spelling and grammar. The two halves, together, form a whole; the story of the pioneers of street railways in the formative years of the nineteenth century.

Neither has any attempt been made here to re-tell Train's life story. He dictated his autobiography from memory, and there are several biographies to which the inquiring reader is directed. They have to be read with reserve, if his memories relating to his non-tramway activities are as selective as those which have been questioned in the unravelling of this facet of his life.

Alan W Brotchie
Aberdour, Scotland
January 2014

PART ONE

Pioneers of Street Railways in
the USA ... and elsewhere

John R Stevens

Street Railway Company button
with American and British flags
(Collection of Ashley Birch)

Acknowledgements

I have had much valued assistance from a number of people who have helped in the collection of information from which this monograph was prepared. Allen Morrison of New York was particularly helpful in directing me to 19th century printed sources, and for the translation of French texts. My thanks also go to Leo Baunsgaard of Copenhagen, Denmark; James Guilbeau of New Orleans; Louis Hennick of Shreveport, Louisiana; Jacques Henry of Paris, France; Bruce Holcomb of Taipalsaari, Finland; Robert Jones of Wallasey, England; Ken McCarthy of Keiraville, Australia; Don Mueller of Milwaukee, Wisconsin; John Price of London, England; and John White, Jr., of Oxford, Ohio.

Libraries that have been a valuable resource are the Engineering Societies Library in New York (no longer in existence); the New York Public Library, and in particular its rare book and manuscript division; the library of the Museum of the City of New York; the Yale University Library and the Benieke rare book library at Yale, in New Haven, Connecticut. Also to be mentioned are the Notarial Archives in New Orleans; New Orleans Public Library; the Historic New Orleans Collection; the Southeastern Architectural Archive at Tulane University, New Orleans.

Map of the City of New York produced in 1835 by Henry A. Tanner, Philadelphia. This shows the line of the N.Y. & H.R.R. with its south end on Park Row by the Hall of Records. The line did not extend this far south until three years after the date of the map. (John R. Stevens Collection)

Tramways or Street Railways:

The Origins in New York in 1832 – and a Bit Beyond

2010 being the Sesquicentennial Year of the opening of Britain's first street tramway – at Birkenhead on 30th of August 1860, I thought it appropriate to supply some of the background to the street tramway (or street railway as it was known in North America) and in particular to deal with the development of the vehicle used – the tramcar (North American, streetcar).

I. New York & Harlem Rail Road

It is generally given that the first street tramway opened on the 26th of November, 1832 in New York City, which, with a population of about 220,000 was the largest city in the United States. On that date, a mile of standard-gauge single track of a planned double-track line and laid flush with the road surface was put into use on Fourth Avenue (now Park Avenue South) and the Bowery between 14th Street and Prince Street. Two vehicles inaugurated this service – three-compartment carriages modeled after the type of railway carriage then in use in England. More will be said about these.

The line was built by the New York & Harlem Rail Road Company, chartered by the State of New York on the 25th of April, 1831 to build a line from the vicinity of the New York City Hall, mostly on Fourth Avenue except a short section at the south end, below Union Square (14th Street) which was to be on the Bowery. The north end of the line was at the Harlem

River, passing through the Village of Yorkville and terminating at Harlem Village, a distance of about eight miles. This destination was reached in 1838 after extensive engineering work including a deep cutting at 34th Street completed in 1833 and converted to a tunnel in the 1850's. After the cessation of railway service following the opening of Grand Central Terminal in 1872, the tunnel was used by trams – first horse-drawn, and then electric. Since the removal of tram service, it was (and still is) used by automobile traffic. A tunnel was cut through the rock between 90th and 95th Streets at Yorkville, completed in 1837. This tunnel remains in use by trains running in and out of Grand Central Station.

Also chartered at the same time as the New York & Harlem, was the New York & Albany Rail Road which continued to the right-of-way of the New York & Harlem beyond the Harlem River. After the railway had been completed to the Harlem River, this charter was purchased by the New York & Harlem. After a bridge built to Ithiel Town's lattice truss design had been completed, service was extended into the Bronx and Westchester County. White Plains was reached in December, 1844 and Croton Falls in 1848. Thereafter the line was extended to Chatham Four Corners in 1852 where a connection was made with the West Stockbridge and Albany Railroad (later part of the Boston & Albany) for access to the City of Albany, the State Capital. The distance between New York City and Albany is about 150 miles.

Service as far as Harlem was primarily with horses through the late 1830's. Tentative use of steam locomotives commenced in the mid-1830's. On July 1, 1834 an experimental locomotive, a vertical-boiler machine built by William James of New York had a boiler explosion just after leaving Yorkville on its way to New York City, pulling two carriages. By 1839, four steam locomotives were in use, all 4-2-0's built by H. R. Dunham of New York. They were similar to the Norris locomotives bought for use on the Lickey Incline, near Birmingham in England.

On July 4th of 1839, one of the Dunham locomotives, the *New York*, having exceptionally drawn an excursion train as far south as Union Square (14th Street) and having its carriages detached, derailed while in the process of being shunted to the northbound track, While an attempt was being made to re-rail it, its boiler exploded. The engineer and two other persons were instantly killed, and several others seriously injured. Normally, steam locomotives were never operated as far south as 14th Street, 32nd Street being the southern limit of their use. They were never again used south of 32nd Street after this disastrous event.

After the explosion of the *New York*, train cars were individually hauled by horses on the lower part of the line, via Fourth Avenue and the Bowery, Broome Street, Centre Street, terminating at Chatham Street, near the City Hall. In the 1840's a formal station was built on the west side of Fourth Avenue, on the north side of 26th Street. Some double-bogie steam train carriages continued to be horse-hauled to the southern terminus of the line after this date. Steam railway service facilities were built on both sides of Fourth Avenue, just south of the tunnel entrance; engine and car houses, etc. It was at this point that southbound steam-drawn passenger carriages were detached from the locomotives, and drawn by horses to the stations of the two railways using the line. And of course, the reverse for northbound trains.

In 1848, the New York & Harlem became the access to New York for the New York & New Haven Railroad. This company originally had its station on the south side of Canal Street, just east of Broadway –

only a few blocks from the City Hall. A joint freight depot for the New York & Harlem and New York & New Haven was built on the west side of Centre Street, south of Canal Street and in the block immediately north of the notorious 'Tombs' prison. In 1852, the New York & New Haven station was moved to the north half of the block between 26th and 27th Streets owned by the New York & Harlem, and as noted elsewhere was located across the street from the factory of the John Stephenson Company. The joint freight depot on Centre Street remained in use until 1886, and until that date goods wagons were horse-hauled to and from it over tracks that after the opening of Grand Central in 1872 were otherwise exclusively for tram service.

City Line of Cars

Having gone through some background history of the New York & Harlem Railroad, it is pertinent now to deal with that aspect of its operation that can be specifically designated as a tramway. In the New York & Harlem minutes is a committee report of November 21, 1837 stating that one track of the railway was complete from Walker Street (several blocks south of Prince Street in the Bowery) to 125th Street. Cars were running at 20 minute intervals, and it was suggested that cars running between Walker and 42nd Street be run more frequently: 'Your Committee further believes and recommends that four or more cars of a different construction from those now in use be built for the transportation of Passengers from Walker Street to the Locomotive Station. Such cars to be in one compartment with a door on each side [each end?] it appears to your Committee would very much facilitate the receiving and landing [of] passengers and collecting their fare.'

'A motion was made by the President that the Locomotives run between 32nd Street and Harlem and that 32nd Street be considered the starting place by Steam.'

'The Vice President stated that the Granite rails in [the] Bowery and 4th Avenue were very defective and that in consequence thereof the cars were daily receiving considerable injury. He therefore moved that the said granite rails be taken up and that wood be substituted [Note: Franz Anton, Ritter von Gerstner in his *Innern Communicationen in Amerika,* published posthumously in Vienna, 1842–3, described and illustrated the granite rail construction] ... The President then moved that the part between 13th and 14th Streets be laid with grove [sic. grooved] rail ...'

On May 4, 1838 it is recorded that the Common Council of the City granted authority to extend rails south to Chatham Street opposite the Hall of Records. Rails 'similar to those laid between 13th and 14th Streets by a double track from the Bowery through Broome Street to Centre Street to Chatham Street ...' After this was done, track on the Bowery south of Broome Street to Walker Street was to be taken up.

On October 18, 1838 a separate tramway operation was referred to as the '27th Street Line', to be run on a ten minute schedule between 8 a.m. and 6 p.m. In November, the frequency was reduced to 15 minutes. On December 17, 1842 the 'City Hall and 27th Street Line' cars had the ten minute schedule restored.

In September, 1841 a New York & Harlem report lists 31 passenger cars. Ten of these were double-bogie carriages of which five were 'diamond' type-Stephenson-built with lattice-truss sides. One 'three coach body' car was still on the roster. More importantly for our tramway interest are twenty 'square five minute cars' for the City Hall to 27th Street service. In 1845 there were 26 'City Line Cars'. By 1859 there were 42 of these vehicles.

The first mention of the coach and railway carriage manufacturing firm of Eaton, Gilbert at Troy, New York in the New York & Harlem minutes is on February 4, 1846 when the Vice President was authorized to contract with them for three, 56 passenger carriages, one of them to have a 'Ladies Apartment''. On April 5, 1847 the President was authorized to contract for 'four additional Passenger cars *and 4 City Cars*'. The name of the supplier of this equipment is not given, but was possibly Eaton, Gilbert. It would have been nice if this information had been revealed since if it was Eaton, Gilbert that was referred to, it would have been the first reference to their construction of tram cars.

On May 20, 1848 a committee was appointed to petition the Common Council to allow the railway to extend its tracks from Chatham Street, down Park Row to Broadway, opposite the Tremont Hotel and adjacent St. Paul's Chapel. City permission to construct this track was given on February 7, 1851.

By 1852, a tramway service had been run by the New York & Harlem for more than ten years from adjacent to the City Hall to their station at 26th Street.

During this period of time a specialized vehicle had evolved for the service. Illustrations of some of these early horse trams have been located. Starting in 1846, the New York & Harlem started purchasing rolling stock from the Eaton, Gilbert & Company of Troy, New York, an industrial city on the east side of the Hudson River about ten miles north of the State Capital at Albany. By 1852, vehicles built by Eaton, Gilbert had developed into the recognizable form of a tramcar, and the stage was set was the introduction of street tramways on a large scale.

Octagonal copper token for the New York & Harlaem (*sic*) Railroad Company. B&S indicates the maker, Bale & Smith.

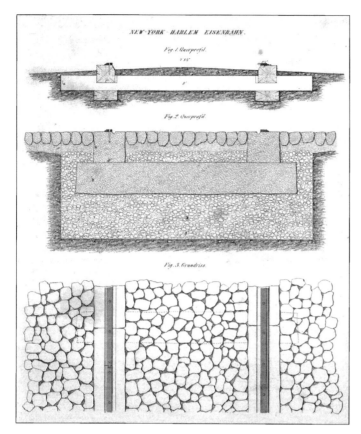

Left. Track construction in the early period of the N.Y. & H.R.R. Fig. 1 shows the construction on unpaved roads, using wooden sleepers and stringers. Fig. 2, 3 show the construction on paved streets using granite 'sills' and sleepers. In both cases, iron rails served as the running surface. From Plate 17 in *Die Innern Communicationen der Vereinigten Staaten von Nord Amerika* … by Franz Anton Ritter von Gerstner, Vienna 1842–3. (Beneicke Rare Book Library, Yale University, New Haven, Connecticut)

Below. Northbound City Line car of the N.Y. & H.R.R. in front of St. Philip's Church on Centre Street. The 'Tombs' prison is shown at the right. Line engraving in *The Evergreen*, Vol. VI, February 1849. (Beneicke Rare Book Library, Yale University, New Haven, Connecticut)

Left. City Line car of the N.Y. & H.R.R. passing the Astor Place Theatre. From *Views of New-York* by Henry Hoff, 1850. (New York Public Library)

Below. Fourth Avenue looking north from 32nd Street. Murray Hill tunnel (which still exists) in the distance. Shows facilities for servicing steam locomotives on the west side of street. Steam locomotives were taken off the trains here, and the carriages were horse-drawn to the passenger depots between 26th and 27th Streets. Wood engraving in the *Boston Illustrated Magazine*, May 23, 1857. (Library of Congress, Washington, D.C.)

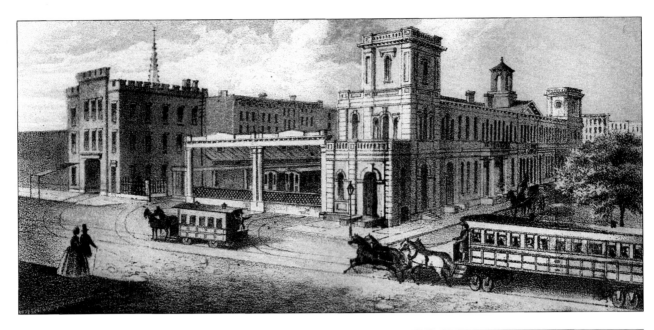

Top. 'Rail-Road Depot in 4th. Ave ...' Actually two depots – New York & Harlem on the left, and New York & New Haven on the right. They occupied the block from 26th to 27th Streets, between Fourth and Madison Avenues. At its opening in 1848, the N.Y. and N.H. depot was farther down town, on Canal Street. The depot on 27th Street was across the street from the John Stephenson Company omnibus and tramcar manufactory. Lithograph from D. T. Valentine's *Manual of the City and Corporation of New York*, 1860.

Above. View in Fourth Avenue, looking north-west from the intersection of 26th Street showing the former depot buildings of the N.Y. & H. and N.Y. & N.H. railroads as converted to the first Madison Square Garden, formerly the Hippodrome. (From the New York Life Company, whose head office has occupied this site since 1928, following the demolition of the second Madison Square Garden)

Joint freight depot of the N.Y. & H. and N.Y. & N.H. railroads. View from the south east. It was on the west side of Centre Street, between White and Franklin Streets. The 'Tombs' prison occupied the block to the south. The upper floors at the south end were occupied from 1853 by E. Anthony, manufacturer of photographic supplies and publisher of stereographic views. These premises were destroyed by fire in April, 1856. A photograph exists of the damaged building. (From an E. Anthony advertisement 1856, John R. Stevens collection)

Fourth Avenue looking north from Union Square (14th Street). The middle track is occupied by a horse-drawn box car on its way north from the joint freight depot of the N.Y. & H. and N.Y. & N.H. railroads on Centre Street. The freight depot was in use until the mid-1880's. Photograph c.1870.

New York & Harlem Railroad tram No. 49, a John Stephenson Company product, on Fourth Avenue near 10th Street. Photograph c.1865.

JOHN STEPHENSON.
THE VETERAN CAR BUILDER—BORN JULY 4, 1809, DIED JULY 31, 1893.
(See page 549.)

Engraved portrait of John Stephenson, from a photograph. Used in the *Street Railway Journal* with his obituary in 1893.

II. John Stephenson

John Stephenson was born in County Armagh, Northern Ireland in 1809. When he was two, his parents emigrated to the United States, settling in New York. At the age of 19, he was apprenticed to coachbuilder, Andrew Wade. Abram Brower, an operator of coaches who purchased vehicles from Wade, became impressed with Stephenson's skill and encouraged the young man to set up his own shop, which Brower allowed him to do in one of his stables. So, in 1831 John Stephenson had a coach building shop up and running, and soon had an order from Brower to construct a vehicle for city service – taken from an idea then current in Paris and London. The coach, which had a rear entrance and seats along its sides had OMNIBUS lettered on its upper side panels.

And what concerns us more here, is that also in 1831, Stephenson was given an order to build railway carriages for the newly chartered New York & Harlem Rail Road. In 1833, he was granted a United States patent for certain improvements to the design of railway carriages, notably an arrangement to have the wheels come up under the seats to lower the floor level. This covered both compartment-type vehicles (as illustrated in the patent drawing, which shows a three-compartment vehicle, obviously based on English railway carriages of the time) and end entrance, side seat vehicles. The original patent, signed by President Andrew Jackson, is preserved in the library of New York University. It can be assumed, I would suppose, that these improvements were incorporated into the vehicle(s) that Stephenson constructed for the New York & Harlem, but can we be sure?

Stephenson prospered at the building of railway carriages, not only for the New York & Harlem, but for a number of other companies as well. He developed a design for double-bogie passenger carriages, the side wall construction of which was based on Ithiel Town's lattice truss design for bridges. Because of the shape of the windows, these were called 'diamond' carriages. A fine large factory was built on the west side of the New York & Harlem line at 129th Street in Harlem. One of America's periodic financial collapses in 1842 put Stephenson into bankruptcy. The purchasers of his railway carriages did not have the cash to pay for them.

However, Stephenson managed a quick recovery, building a multi-storeyed factory on the north side of East 27th Street, immediately west of Fourth Avenue (now Park Avenue South). There was a brick wall along the street, with an arched opening in it, and a large courtyard behind it fronting the factory. The courtyard was used for the preparation of vehicles for shipping, and some were taken through the archway to be photographed partly on the street, and partly on the pavement. On the south side of 27th Street, and down to 26th Street was the station and storage yard of the New York & Harlem. In about 1852, the north half of the block had built on it a station for the New York & New Haven Railroad, which thereby was right across the street from the Stephenson factory. The construction of railway carriages was abandoned and Stephenson concentrated all his production on building omnibuses for which there was a big demand in New York and other American cities.

In the mid-1850's, Stephenson was approached by the President of the Third Avenue Railroad Company to produce a tramcar lighter that those currently in use, which Stephenson deemed 'real horse killers'. What he built was a hybrid tram-omnibus, the body of which was almost identical to the omnibuses he was building, but a bit wider.

He also had the idea of mounting the body on the running gear in a way that allowed the body to rotate on top of it. Thus was created the first reversible-bodied tramcar, a design that became popular in Britain in the 1870's by the version designed and patented by John Eades. Two of Stephenson's reversible-bodied trams have managed to survive – one from the Eighth Avenue Railroad, which was exhibited at the Museum of the City of New York for many years. After a period in storage, it was recently transferred to the New York Transit Museum in the former Court Street subway station. The other, which was built for use in Chicago, but at an early date was sold to Omaha, Nebraska where it became the first tram to run there. This is displayed at Harold Warp's Pioneer Village, at Minden, Nebraska.

Stephenson did not get into the large-scale manufacture of tramcars in addition to his major product, omnibuses, until the end of the 1850's. An elevation drawing of a car produced in 1857 shows a vehicle very much like those used in New York and other American cities – bearing in mind that at this time hundreds of horse-drawn trams were in use, many if not most built by the Eaton, Gilbert firm of Troy (the subject of another section of this work). In the late 1850's, new builders of tramcars were established in Philadelphia: Kimball & Gorton and Murphy & Allison. The distinctive body design of these trams provided the design for Birkenhead's first trams, and imported vehicles from this source were used on George Francis Train's London tramways of 1861.

Stephenson rapidly developed a design for a lighter-weight conventional tramcar. An improvement he introduced was to have separate platform hoods

rather than the main roof structure being extended beyond the bulkheads. The present whereabouts of the Stephenson order books, if they exist, is not known. There was an exhibition at the Museum of the City of New York in 1945 on John Stephenson that displayed many artifacts – photographs, models, drawings and account books. The museum has not been able to locate for me an inventory of this exhibit, but it is possible that the account books in the display may have been the company order books?

The closest thing to an order book reference, I found at the New-York Historical Society. This is a letter dated November 17, 1882 from John Stephenson to J. R. Butler, the President of the Sixth Avenue Railroad. This makes reference to pages in an order book, for cars supplied to the Sixth Avenue company between 1860 and 1866. Most revealing is the comment on the first entry, for January 1860: 'I car, two horse No. 45 Weight 3578 lbs. (First car with bonnet [platform hood] – Experiment)'.

Trams supplied to New Orleans in 1860 show the fully-developed body design that persisted almost to the end of horse haulage of tramcars. These New Orleans cars were single-ended with the front platform for the driver having a 'wrap-around' dash. At the rear was an omnibus step for the passengers. A farebox was built into the front bulkhead into which passengers deposited their fares, and a slide in the door allowed the driver to pass change through. A lever arrangement permitted the driver to open and close the rear door. Small turntables in the street were used to reverse direction of these cars.

We do not have much information about the Stephenson product line in the 1860's but he evidently prospered greatly. The factory production during the American Civil War, 1861–1865, was heavily involved in war materiel, such as gun carriages. Historic Richmond Town on Staten Island (a Borough of New York City) possesses one of the gun carriages the Stephenson firm manufactured.

John Stephenson became very rich from the production of tramcars, omnibuses and war materiel. He got rather carried away with his new affluence when in the mid-1860's he built a magnificent towered mansion on the north shore of Long Island Sound, a little east of the City of New Rochelle in Westchester County, New York. This property was named 'Clifford'. Stephenson used company funds for the construction of his mansion, to the detriment of the company. The result was that management of the company was taken out of his hands, although it retained his name, and he was given the title of President, which he retained for the rest of his life.

With plenty of time on his hands, being freed from the day-to-day running of the company, John Stephenson became something of a company 'elder statesman' and spokesperson. Interviews with him, and reports on him and the company appeared with some frequency in trade publications like *Engineering, Railway Age, Scientific American, Street Railway Journal*, etc. It was about this time that Stephenson made the claim that he had been the builder of 'the original street car' in 1831. That he had in fact ridden on it at the opening ceremonies of the New York & Harlem in the company of the Mayor and members of the Common Council of the City of New York. Stephenson neglected to note that the vehicle he produced was only one of the two used on this auspicious occasion!

A wood engraving of the 'Original Street Car' began to be used for publicity purposes by the Stephenson company in the 1870's. The earliest use of it I have seen is in a full-page advert in *Longworth's New York City Directory* for 1871–72. While similar to the patent drawing of 1833, it does not show top-seats for passengers – only baggage security rails along the sides of the roof. On the other hand, the patent drawing shows three pairs of back-to-back roof seats, apparently the full width of the roof, with the end seats being used by the driver (or brakeman). No means of access to these seats is shown. The account in the *Railroad Journal* in November 1832 states that the roofs of both cars were used for accommodation of passengers.

In the engraving, the name *JOHN MASON* appears over the center door of the three-compartment carriage. The patent drawing has the name *President* written in this location, and on Stephenson's own testi-mony in the December 1832 issue of the *Railroad Journal, President* was the name of the car he supplied to the New York & Harlem that was used at the opening ceremony. A photograph taken inside the Stephenson factory in the early 1890's shows, fairly high on a wall, a large framed drawing, titled the ORIGINAL STREET CAR. The present location of this drawing is not known.

It is to be noted that the wood engraving from the 1870's of the *JOHN MASON* as described above was not the first reproduced version of this image. Without lettering, a wood engraved image said to have been produced by Alexander Robb of Philadelphia began to be used as a 'stock cut' for railway timetables and such like in the later 1830's. This version was of a steam railway carriage with a brakeman on one of the end roof seats. Passengers are shown in the windows. A much reduced version of the image was used on one side of tickets used by the New York & Harlem Rail Road, with the lettering underneath, RAIL ROAD CAR.

In the late 1860's, the Stephenson firm developed a design for top-seat trams in order to get into the market for such vehicles for tramways being opened in Britain, Continental Europe and South America. In the Stephenson collection of photographs in the Museum of the City of New York there are three photographs showing the original design elements. Access to the top seats was gained by a removable ladder which hooked to the edge of a platform hood and at the bottom was attached to the draft gear. It must have been a very awkward job, indeed, for the driver and conductor to detach the ladder and manhandle it around to the other end of the car when reversing direction!

It is known that cars with ladders were supplied by Stephenson to London in 1870, but there are no illustrations of a London car so equipped, except for one in a French publication. The car body shown in this illustration does not correspond with Stephenson practice, however.

One of the three photographs mentioned is of a car built as a special order for an entrepreneur for a Glasgow line, 'Cross to Anderston'. No evidence has been found that it was ever used in that city. It had a

12 foot (six window) car body which was narrower than standard – in fact, the car's sides were flat. Its built-up wheels were without flanges; nor were brakes present. Advertisements offering this vehicle for sale appeared in Glasgow newspapers over an extended period of time. These have only recently been discovered, along with a photograph of this very tram in use in Stirling, Scotland. For use there, it had been equipped with regular iron wheels and brakes. It had proper quarter-turn stairs and knifeboard top-seats.

Stephenson soon realized the inadequacy of the ladder arrangement, and went one better than the spiral iron ladders used by British tramcar manufacturers like George Starbuck in Birkenhead, and Metropolitan Railway Carriage and Wagon, at Birmingham. In 1871, Stephenson supplied a single 16 foot (8 window) car, No. 5, to Leeds Tramway with fully-developed quarter-turn stairs – a design which in the 1870's was adopted by British and other tramcar manufacturers. I suspect that the cars Stephenson supplied to London with ladders, were rebuilt with proper stairs supplied as 'kits', consisting of new platforms, hoods and stairs.

Stephenson supplied omnibuses and tramcars to systems around the World. Some of the builders' photographs show crated car bodies in the courtyard of the 27th Street factory. For shipment, the platforms and platform hoods were removed and presumably put inside the body. I suspect that the running gear was crated separately.

Several Stephenson top-seat trams have survived in near-original condition in Australia and New Zealand, and in both of these countries there are preserved locally-built top-seat trams that are almost exact copies of the New York-built ones. Two top-seat Stephenson trams for London have survived. One is displayed fully restored at the London Transport Museum at Covent Garden, a 14 foot (7 window) car with the number 284. The body of an identical car still on its running gear is at the National Tramway Museum at Crich. However, these two cars had been rebuilt by London Tramways in about 1890 with 'garden seats' [transverse double seats] as an improvement over the original knifeboard ones. The rebuilding was fairly drastic, and

involved the complete replacement of the roof structure between the bulkheads. There is a photograph of No. 284 as built, with knifeboard top-seats in the collection of Stephenson builders' pictures at the Museum of the City of New York.

John Stephenson died in 1893 at the age of 84. His wife, Julia Tiemann, predeceased him by two years. They are buried at the Stephenson plot at Beechwood Cemetery in New Rochelle. The Stephenson mansion, 'Clifford' was acquired by the Roman Catholic order of Don Bosco Salesians in 1918, and continues in use as their regional headquarters.

At the time of John Stephenson's death, the firm was the largest builder of tramcars in the World. The factory building on East 27th Street with its multiple storeys and low head room was hardly ideal for the production of horse trams, and totally inadequate for the manufacture of electric trams. Other manufacturers were in competition – like the J. G. Brill Company in Philadelphia; J. M. Jones' Sons in West Troy New York; St. Louis and American Car companies in St. Louis, Missouri. The Stephenson firm was reorganized and a new factory built at Elizabeth, New Jersey, but it was not successful. In the end, Stephenson, American Car, and other tramcar manufacturers were taken over by the Brill company which succeeded to the title of being the largest manufacturer of tramcars in the World.

Brass slide for change from door of early Stephenson-built horse car (see lower illustration on page 21).

The Schedule referred to in these Letters Patent, & making parts of the same, containing a description in the words of the said John Stephenson himself of his improvements in Passenger Cars for rail-ways.

To all whom these presents shall come:

Be it known that I John Stephenson of the City & County of New York & State of New York have invented a new and useful improvement in Passenger Cars for Railways, & that the following is a full & exact description of the same as invented by me …

The bottom of the body is made with openings suffi-cient to admit the wheels up into the body under the seats, which are in all cases, over the wheels, either running & parallel, to the sides of the body, or crosswise, as may be expedient.

*The carriage part is suspended under the axles having the boxes **A**. or bearings, bolted or otherwise fastened on the top side of the Carriage … on the top of each of the boxes or bearings, is fastened a leather brace **B**. the brace may be two feet long, four inches wide & two thick, the size of the brace may vary to suit convenience or drawn tight at either end by a screw **C**. of suitable size running thro' the pillars of the body **D**. or goose necks **E**. under the bottom side rails (this mode of hanging the body is applicable to stages and other Carriages.) … It will be seen that by making the*

body as above specified, it is brought down almost as low as the axles … The doors of the body open down to the bottom of the side rails.

The principles of improvement consist of admitting the wheels up thro' the bottom & the method of hanging the body as specified above

Witnesses   *John Stephenson*
Joseph Carnwell
Wm. I. Dodge

Printed receipt for $30.00 attached to page. '**In conformity** to an act of Congress entitled An act to promote the progress of the useful arts, approved 21st February, 1793, I have received of *John Stephenson* THIRTY DOLLARS which sum has been placed to the credit of my account in the Branch Bank at *Washington* under the date of *17th April 1833* and for this I have signed duplicate receipts.

John Campbell
Treasurer of the United States'

Copy of original document and transcription supplied by the late Don Mueller. The original document and the side elevation of the vehicle are in the library of New York University in New York City.

John Stephenson's patent drawing, 1833. The car is named 'President' over the middle door. (Original drawing at New York University. Copy from the Museum of the City of New York)

Left. Carriage of Stephenson patent design. Wood engraving by Alexander Robb of Philadelphia that was used in advertisements in the 1830's. (Broadside in the collections of Old Sturbridge Village, Sturbridge Massachusetts)

Below. Stephenson patent carriages, Philadelphia & Columbia Railroad, 1834. This model of a train was exhibited at the Columbian Exposition at Chicago in 1893, and is now at the Railroad Museum of Pennsylvania at Strasburg.

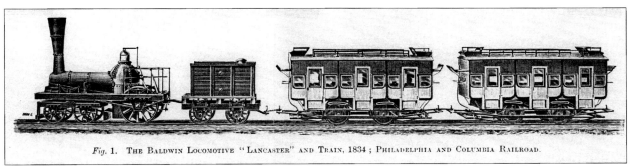

Fig. 1. THE BALDWIN LOCOMOTIVE "LANCASTER" AND TRAIN, 1834; PHILADELPHIA AND COLUMBIA RAILROAD.

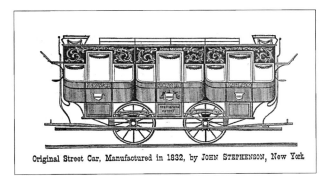

Original Street Car, Manufactured in 1832, by JOHN STEPHENSON, New York

Left. Wood engraving of the 'Original Street Car Manufactured in 1832, by John Stephenson, New York'. From an advertisement in a New York City directory, 1873.

Below left. Reversible-bodied horsecar No. 76 of the Eighth Avenue Railroad, New York built by the John Stephenson Company in the 1850's. View from the front. (Museum of the City of New York)

Below right. As last, view from the rear. The body is similar to the omnibuses built by the Stephenson company, but somewhat wider. (Museum of the City of New York)

Stephenson reversible-bodied horsecar No. 1 of the Omaha, Nebraska Street Railway ex Chicago, Illinois. Side and rear views. This vehicle is in the collections of Harold Warp's Pioneer Village at Minden, Nebraska. (Henry Hamman Collection, Western Heritage Museum, Omaha Nebraska)

Left. Interior of Omaha No. 1, looking towards the front. (Henry Hamman Collection, Western Heritage Museum, Omaha Nebraska)

Below. Drawings of a Stephenson reversible-bodied horsecar. Plate 2 of *Aufsatze Betreffend Das Eisenbahnwesen in Nord Amerika* ... A. Bendel, Berlin 1862. (Yale University Library, New Haven Connecticut)

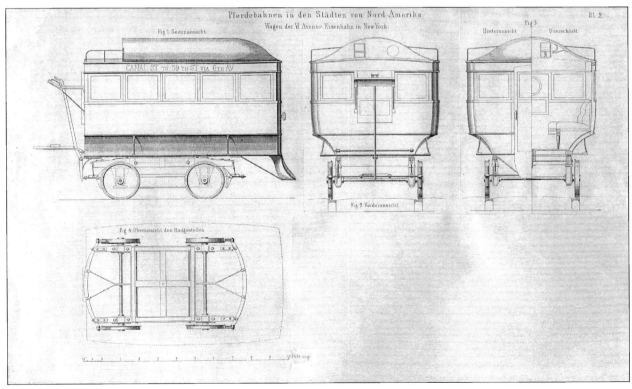

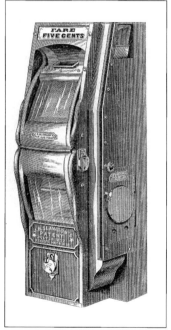

Top. An early standard-bodied horsecar built by the Stephenson company in the 1860's for Milwaukee, Wisconsin before a standard body design had evolved. Shown as later modified as a single-end farebox car. (Don Mueller collection)

Lower left. Canal Street, New Orleans Louisiana, 1860. Stephenson's first 'Bob Tail' trams (single-end farebox cars). This photograph was taken shortly after the opening of the New Orleans City Railroad. (Historic New Orleans Collection)

Lower right. John B. Slawson's patent farebox. Engraving from the *Street Railway Journal* c.1890.

Typical (except for its running gear) New Orleans City Railroad 14 foot body, one-man bob-tail horsecar No. 73, built by the John Stephenson Company in 1868. View from the front. (Collections of the Museum of the City of New York)

Rear view of above car No. 73. (Collections of the Museum of the City of New York)

Interior view, looking towards the front, of this car, showing the 'CHANGE' slide in the door, and to the right of it the Slawson farebox. Note the instructions for the use of the farebox pasted on the inside of the glass (see illus. opposite). (Collections of the Museum of the City of New York)

Top right. A special-order tram with a 12 foot body built by the Stephenson Company for the entrepreneurs of a proposed line in Glasgow, Scotland. It has experimental running gear (also shown on previous page). The patent date on the running gear is May 23, 1867. The wheels do not have flanges nor is there evidence of brakes. Note the ladder access to the top seats which can be shifted from one end of the car to the other. (Collections of the Museum of the City of New York)

Middle right. Typical Stephenson omnibus for Melbourne, Australia. The Glasgow tram can be seen through the archway into the courtyard of the Stephenson factory. (Collections of the Museum of the City of New York)

Below. The tram shown above ended up in Stirling, Scotland. For use there it was given new running gear, platforms, stairs and top-seats. (A. W. Brotchie)

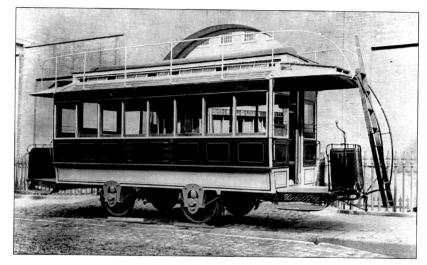

Top-seat tram supplied by the John Stephenson Company to London, c.1870? 16 foot body tram with a shifting ladder for top-seat access. At this time, the Starbuck Company at Birkenhead was supplying top-seat trams with quarter-turn spiral iron stairs at both ends. Unusual running gear pedestals are shown. (Collections of the Museum of the City of New York)

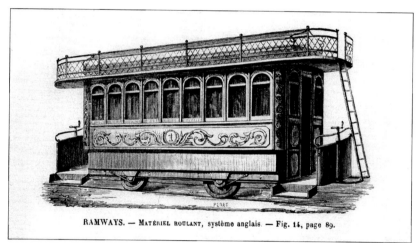

RAMWAYS. — Matériel roulant, système anglais. — Fig. 14, page 89.

Engraving of 'Rolling stock, English system' showing a top-seat tram with this type of shifting ladder. From: *Etude sur Chemins de Fer Les Tramways.* F. Serafon, Paris 1872) (Yale University Library, New Haven, Connecticut)

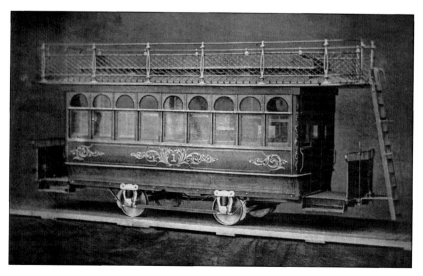

Print from a glass negative acquired by A. W. Brotchie in 2010, apparently the source of the above engraving. The model has a Philadelphia-style body and running gear. An unusual feature is the railing extending round the platform hoods.

Top-seat tram supplied by the Stephenson Company to Leeds, in 1871. 16 foot body. The fully-developed stair has arrived! Note the narrow 'knife board' which serves as a back for the top-seats. (Collections of the Museum of the City of New York)

Top-seat tram supplied by the Stephenson Company to Liverpool, in 1875. 14 foot body. Here, the top-seats have a fully-developed form. Note the hemp mats on the platform hoods which supply non-slip access to the footboards along the top deck. (Collections of the Museum of the City of New York)

Top-seat tram No. 284 supplied by the Stephenson Company to the London Tramways Company, c.1883. 14 foot body. Wood-slat mats on the platform hoods have replaced the hemp versions shown above. A tram numbered 284 is preserved at the London Transport Museum. This has a different roof construction, and if it is the vehicle shown here, the roof structure was replaced by a new arrangement of 'garden seats' on either side of a narrow central aisle. (Collections of the Museum of the City of New York)

Top. The John Stephenson Company factory at 45-47 East 27th Street, New York c.1889, from the south. The rubble in the foreground is the remains of the New York & New Haven Railroad depot, which, after the opening of Grand Central Station at 42nd Street in 1872 was transformed into Barnum's Hippodrome, which later became the first Madison Square Garden (see page 10). A new Madison Square Garden was built on the site, which lasted until 1926 when it was demolished, and replaced by the headquarters building of the New York Life Company which still occupies the site. The electric tram for Omaha, Nebraska has a body like the Roundhay, Leeds electric trams supplied from the U.S.A. in 1891, possibly built by Stephenson. (Collections of the Museum of the City of New York)

Above left. John Stephenson's mansion 'Clifford' at New Rochelle, New York from which he could conveniently get to his factory in New York on the New York & New Haven Railroad. Built in the 1860's at a cost said to have been about $250,000.00, an enormous amount of money for a house at that time. Since 1919 it has been owned by the Roman Catholic Salesian Order of Don Bosco. Seen from the south west. (John R. Stevens photograph)

Above right. Gravestone in Beechwood Cemetery, New Rochelle, New York, for John Stephenson, July 4, 1809 to July 31, 1893 and his wife, Julia A. Tieman, March 3, 1811 to February 27, 1891. (John R. Stevens photograph)

25

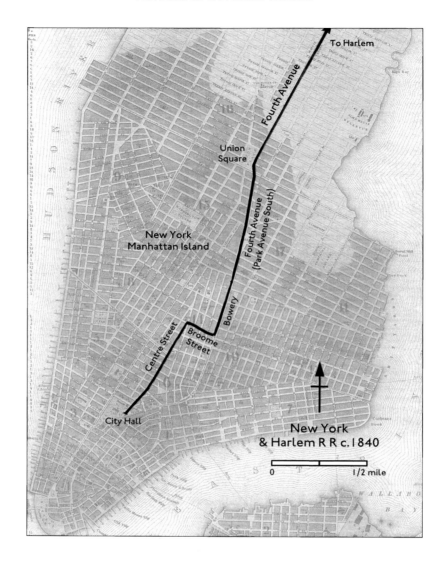

III. Miln Parker and the First Railway Carriages of the New York & Harlem Rail Road

In Volume One of the *Railroad Journal*, published by D. Kimball Minor in New York, in the issue for November 17, 1832 the lead article commenced as follows:

'We were gratified on Wednesday last, as we were passing up the Bowery, with a view of the beautiful cars of the Harlaem Railroad Company. We understand they were made by Mr. Miln Parker, coach-maker, of this city.

They are spacious and convenient, being divided into three distinct apartments, each amply large enough for eight, and can accommodate very conveniently ten persons – or twenty-four to thirty passengers inside; and when we saw them, there were at least, we should think, an equal number upon, and hanging around the outside, the whole being drawn by two fine horses abreast, at the rate of ten to twelve miles an hour. We admired their construction, and believe they are less liable to accident than most others we have seen, as the wheels are under the body...'

It is to be noted that this, and subsequent issues of this publication dealt with steam carriages on common roads – a hot topic in Britain at the time. The New York & Harlem Rail Road officially opened on November 26, 1832 – nine days after the date of this issue of the *Railroad Journal*.

The issue of the *Railroad Journal* for December 1, 1832 contains the following:

'CREDIT TO WHOM CREDIT IS DUE –
In our notice a short time since the opening of the Haerlem Railroad for use, we spoke of the beautiful Cars upon it as having been built by Mr. Miln Parker, and so we at the time supposed, from what we heard, was the fact. We have since learned, however, that one of them, the *President*, was built by Mr. Stephenson, coach-maker, at 264 Elizabeth Street, New York.'

So, contrary to John Stephenson's claim, made in the 1870's that he had built 'the Original Street Car', in fact he was the supplier of only one of the two vehicles seen used at this event prior to the official opening of the line. The two vehicles must have looked remarkably alike for the editorial writer of the Railroad Journal to have mistakenly thought them to have been the product of a single builder!

Of course, the idea that these vehicles were tramcars/streetcars was stretching the truth a bit. They were seen in use on paved track in the upper part of New York City, but the intention in building the New York & Harlem was to extend it, on the right-of-way of Fourth Avenue, to the north end of Manhattan Island, at the Harlem River. Horse-power was initially used, but within a short time the service to Harlem was by coupled carriages hauled by steam locomotives. Until replaced with double-bogie carriages, four-wheel ones like those built by Miln Parker and John Stephenson were for a time in use with steam locomotives.

About Miln Parker, little is recorded. He shows up in *Longworth's New York Directory* for 1820–21 as a coachmaker and repository at Broadway and Spring Streets in New York City. In 1828–29, his shop was located in Yorkville. By the mid-1830's Parker shows up as a land broker, and later as an auctioneer. The last entry for him that I found, 1844–45 has him as a public magistrate.

The Minutes of the New York & Harlem Rail Road, in the Rare Book and Manuscript Collection of the New York Public Library show approximately equal payments being made to Miln Parker and John Stephenson for the rolling stock they supplied. On September 6, 1833 it was noted that Parker had four cars 'nearly finished'. In 1834, on April 18th the following is noted: 'to buy cars *New York* ($1,050) and *Ohio* ($1,258) from Miln Parker'.

From November 1832 to October 1836, payments of $5,057 are recorded to John Stephenson and $6,733 to Miln Parker. The only other car builder named in these early accounts was Messrs. M. P. & M. E. Green of Hoboken, New Jersey, which firm received $5,721 between April 1834 and July 1836.

In May, 1833 there were '6 good cars' on the New York & Harlem roster; in February 1837 the company President reported that seventeen cars were in use.

Stephenson car shown at the 1867 Paris Exposition, showing top deck access by ladder. The India Street Railway Coy named on the car has not been traced, but an Indian Tramway Coy Ltd was floated in London in 1862. Despite grand intentions, it only built one 18 mile long line of 3 ft 6 ins gauge (steam powered) from Arconum on the Madras Railway to Conjeveram (now Arakkonam to Kanchipuram).

Map of the street
railway lines of the
New Orleans &
Carrollton Railroad
showing the situation
in April, 1836.
(Drawn by Louis C.
Hennick, 2010)

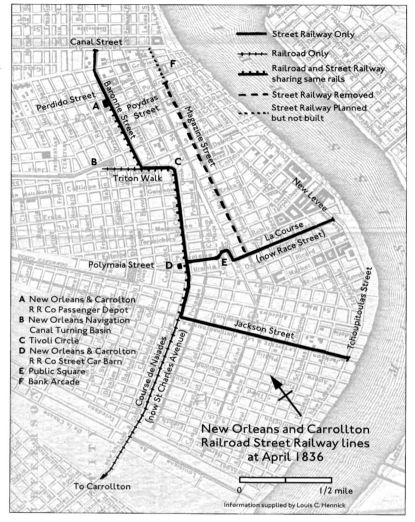

IV. The First True Street Railway –
Magazine Street, New Orleans, Louisiana
Contributed by Louis C. Hennick

The year 2010 was the 175th Anniversary of tramway/streetcar service in New Orleans, and portions of today's St. Charles line were part of the 1835 installation. Although the New York & Harlem Railroad operation that commenced in November 1832 has been credited as being the first tramway/street railway operation (see section I.), this distinction more properly applies to the Magazine Street line of the New Orleans & Carrollton Railroad. Here, three years

after the opening of the New York & Harlem's operation on Fourth Avenue and the Bowery, Civil Engineer Charles F. Zimpel (see section V.) planned the first true street railway designed to provide a specialized service to the Public.

By early 1834 the New Orleans & Carrollton Railroad's Charter and Amendments had met with the approval of the New Orleans City Council and the Louisiana State Legislature. The State Capital was in New Orleans at that time. The N.O. & C.R.R.Co. proposed to build two 'street railroad' lines in the City of New Orleans (the Charter's terminology used that phrase, but by 1835 the nomenclature had changed to 'street railway' and newspapers had adopted the term 'streetcar'). One line, the Magazine – LaCourse, was distinct from the rest of the system, while the other, the 'Lafayette' or Jackson Street, used part of the railroad trackage in the middle of its route. The remainder of the N.O. & C.R.R. was a steam railroad (see opposite).

Engineering drawings for the double track on Magazine Street and other portions of trackage, plus various buildings and structures, were Charles F. Zimpel's work, and bear his signature. His drawing of a section of Magazine Street, reproduced with this article, is in the collections of the New Orleans Public Library rare book and manuscript division. The track was to be standard gauge, 4 feet, 8½ inches. Zimpel's specifications called for iron strap rails with a groove ('coulisse') to accommodate railway wheel flanges (see End Note). This configuration prevented free-wheeling street vehicles from jamming their wheels and kept trash, dirt, or stones from filling the space for the wheel flanges. Thus the problem of maintaining a continuous, even street surface was simplified, causing little interference to wagon, buggy or float, or other road vehicles. The rails were fixed to longitudinal wooden stringers, and these in turn were secured to sleepers (see End Note). The Baronne Street portion was single-track in the center, with the same intention as in Magazine Street, to provide a uniform surface allowing vehicles to drive over the rails unimpeded with minimal jolting.

There are two books, expertly researched, covering the early history of the N.O. & C.R.R. and its tramway/street railway lines. In 1927, New Orleans Public Service Inc. published *A Near Century of Public Service in New Orleans*. The author was Hugh Mercer Blain, a Virginian, born December 26, 1874, who removed to Louisiana and became a professor of English at Louisiana State University. There he established the University's Department of Journalism, and completed the book for publication. Much of his sources, such as the Minutes of the Directors' meetings of the N.O. & C.R.R., were in the N.O.P.S.I. archives, where his son Hugh Mercer Blain, Jr. worked. The book was a father-and-son project and an indispensable

source of information for all time. The second book is *The Saint Charles Streetcar* by James Guilbeau, published by the Louisiana Landmarks Society. Mr. Guilbeau is a native New Orleanian, active for many years in historical research and preservation. The first edition of his book appeared in 1975, the second in 1977, and the third edition in 1992. Guilbeau's research brought much new material to light with each revised edition, although the N.O. & C.R.R. minutes were not available, having disappeared in the 1922 fire at the Baronne Street general offices of N.O.P.S.I. It is not known to this day whether these valuable researcher's treasures are in a private collection or perished in the flames. Together, these two books provide an almost complete story of the N.O. & C.R.R. Company from its formation to the present.

It is fortunate that Blain had access to the Minutes. One mystery is solved – the dates that the Magazine – LaCourse, and Jackson Street lines began service. The first weeks of 1835 were devoted to celebrating the 20th anniversary of the Battle of New Orleans. Newspapers are mute over the streetcar lines! However Blain reports 'the Minutes of December 9, 1834 recorded the acceptance of an offer from George Baumgard of "two horses and a driver for the Magazine Street railway car at $4.50 a day".' Next, the Minutes of January 2, 1835 state 'the engineer [Zimpel] authorized to arrange for horses to run on Magazine by contract for no longer than three months'. There was a legal agreement with the City Council in the event a majority of residents and businesses complained the passage of streetcars impeded commerce, the trackage on Magazine Street must be removed and thus the projected continuation of the railway on Magazine from Poydras to Canal Street would not happen. The Jackson Street line had fewer objections, with tracks near the river levee being lowered to the level of the street, and one of the two tracks around the market removed.

The Minutes subsequently stated, in the pages for January 13, 1835, that Zimpel reported 'passenger cars on the Baronne Street route were now running to the head of Jackson Street' (now Jackson Avenue and Tchoupitoulas Street). The fare charged was 12 ½ cents from Canal Street to Tivoli Circle and 18 ¾ cents for the entire trip.

Blain mentioned the origin of the streetcars the N.O. & C.R.R. used at the onset, but Guilbeau's research uncovered more details. He discovered the earliest Minutes of the Pontchartrain Railroad Company's Directors' meetings. In 1831, the P.R.R. ordered four first-class passenger carriages of two-axle, three-compartment configuration the Liverpool & Manchester Railway used, built by the Worsdell father-and-son owned carriage builder proprietorship. When the carriages arrived in New Orleans they were accompanied by a steam locomotive from Britain, and this train commenced steam railway operation in 1832. Two years' later, the N.O. & C.R.R. purchased one of the cars, named 'Orleans', for service on the Magazine Street – LaCourse line. The N.O.&C.R.R. rebuilt the car, added running boards on both sides for access to the compartments, and attached double ladders with safety railings at each end so passengers could reach seats atop the car from either side. A canvas cover shielded passengers on the upper deck from sun and rain. The driver had seats where the ladders met at each end. Each compartment had a door on each side; windows; and facing wooden benches. According to Guilbeau, the company had seven of these hefty cars with roof-top seating in operation by 1835, six having been built at the N.O. & C.R.R. shops in Carrollton (see illustration on page 32).

Guilbeau found an excellent image of one of these cars in the New Orleans Notarial Record of street plans, property lines, building locations. These records have many artistic sketches. A December 1835 painting of a privately built 'Branch of the New Orleans and Carrollton Rail Road, Now in Operation' (on Napoleon and Tchoupitoulas Streets) shows a horse pulling two single-deck passenger cars. A second horse pulls a flat car loaded with freight. There is a photograph of one of the cars taken in 1864, and it is reproduced in Hennick and Charlton's Streetcars of New Orleans, published by Louis C. Hennick in 1965 in New Orleans. By 1868 there were only three of the old double-deck cars in service (according to Blain).

Unfortunately, the Magazine Street double-track between Poydras and LaCourse Streets caused many complaints, and after much acrimony (recorded well in the newspapers) the trackage was removed from that street in late 1835 and relaid on Polymnia Street between Magazine Street and Naiades to keep the line in operation. The new LaCourse line commenced at Canal Street and used the Jackson Street route to Naiades and Polymnia, then on Polymnia, across the Public Square between Camp and Coliseum, then on LaCourse to New Levee Street (now Market Street, one block closer to the Mississippi River from Tchoupitoulas Street). The re-routed line opened in March of 1836 but was closed permanently in the mid 1840's, probably due to omnibus competition.

By the end of the 1840's, New Orleans had a vigorous and comprehensive omnibus network comprising several companies. The N.O. & C.R.R. even had a line, the 'Apollo Street', which connected the N.O. & C.R.R.'s depot with that of the Pontchartrain Railroad, a long through-town service crossing Canal Street. One owner of an omnibus system, the 'Rough and Ready Line', was Mr. J. B. Slawson who invented and patented a revolutionary farebox, and just before the Civil War removed to New York City and joined the John Stephenson car works. Between 1861 and 1868 the Stephenson company delivered hundreds of bob-tail cars to the various street railway companies of New Orleans. These one-man cars were equipped with Slawson fareboxes. In fact, Stephenson bob-tail cars replaced all older NO&CRR streetcars – including the durable double-deckers – in 1868 with a large order of over sixty cars.

The N.O. & C.R.R.Co. was a complete service institution with steam railway passenger and freight; street railway and omnibus lines. Its street railway installation was engineered for that specific purpose on principles still employed today. Tracks on St. Charles Avenue between Lee (formerly Tivoli) Circle to Jackson Avenue, around Lee Circle, and on Howard Avenue between the Circle and Carondelet Street were the precursors of today's St. Charles streetcar line which in 2010 saw its 175th year of city street railway, or tramway, operation. This length of service is a record in and of itself – the World's oldest streetcar line. It is a National Treasure that deserves its place on the United States Department of the Interior's *National Register of Historic Places*, gaining that status on August 4, 1973. The 35 streetcars, built in 1923–24, were undamaged during the flooding of the city in 2005, escaping the fury of hurricane 'Katrina'.

End Note: Charles Zimpel's drawing of a section of Magazine Street is somewhat ambiguous in connection with the actual track construction. The 'rails' are let into the sleepers, which are long enough to carry all four rails. The rails are colored blue, as they also are in the plan view, indicating that they were iron. But their section is too large to represent iron rails. At that time, iron had to be imported from Britain which had the facilities for rolling special sections, but the size of the sections that could be rolled was limited. I suggest that the 'rails' were actually of some hard timber, into which a groove was cut for a flangeway, and on one side of the groove a metal plate about 4 inches wide, and ⅝ – ¾ inch thick was fastened down with screws or spikes, for the treads of the wheels to ride on? This is similar to what was done with the city track of the New York & Harlem Railroad in its 1832 configuration, where the 'rails' were pieces of granite 12 inches square in section and from seven to thirteen feet long with a flangeway cut down the middle of them, and an iron wear strip attached, as just described.

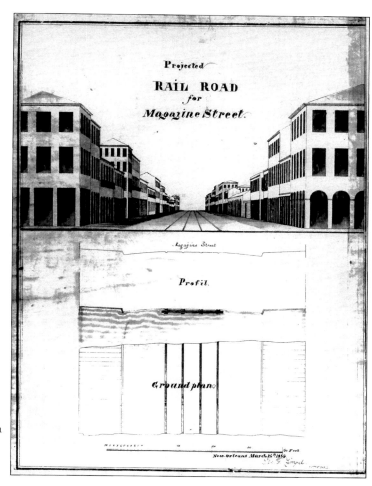

Charles F. Zimpel's drawing, 'Projected Rail Road for Magazine Street' dated New Orleans, March 28th 1834. It shows a plan and section of the street track of the New Orleans & Carrollton Railroad. (New Orleans Public Library, New Orleans, Louisiana)

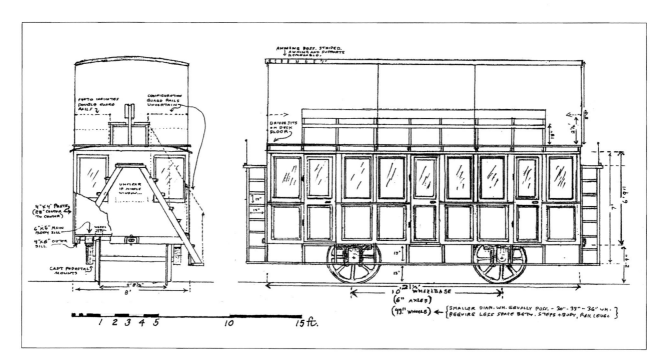

Above. Reconstruction drawing of a top-seat, side-door tram on the New Orleans & Carrollton Railroad. This type of car used from the 1830's to the 1860's. (Drawn by Louis C. Hennick, 2010)

Right. Side elevation and floor plan of a railway carriage for the New Orleans & Carrollton Railroad. Vehicles of this type were built for the railroad by M. P. and M. E. Green, of Hoboken, New Jersey. This firm also built carriages for the New York & Harlem Railroad. From *Das Eisenbahnwesens von Nordamerika, England und Anderen Landen ...* Charles F. Zimpel, Vienna, 1840.

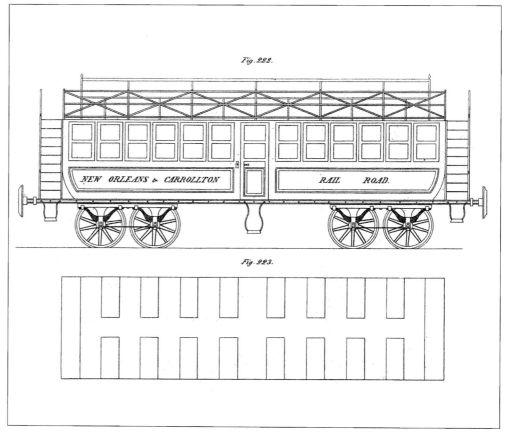

Portrait of Charles F. Zimpel, 1801–1879 in later life.

V. Charles Friedrich Zimpel

Carl Friedrich Zimpel was born in 1801 at Sprottau, Lower Silesia – then in Prussia but now part of Poland. Both of his parents died of tuberculosis when he was quite young, and he suffered from poor health throughout his life. He joined the Prussian Army at the age of 17 and most of his education was obtained during his military service. He was a 'quick learner' in mathematics and engineering, leaving the army after ten years of service with the equivalent of a degree in Engineering.

In 1829 he emigrated to the United States and for a period of time after his arrival in North America is said to have traveled extensively in the United States and in British North America (now Canada). In particular he was interested in the railway development taking place, then in it earliest stages. He settled in New Orleans – a somewhat unusual choice considering the notorious unhealthiness of the place – and became an American citizen. Also, he Anglicized his name to Charles Francis Zimpel. A letter from him concerning railway development that appeared in the New Orleans *Mercantile Advertiser* on July 28, 1831 was signed 'Charles F. Zimpel, Engineer, Architect and Surveyor, late of the Prussian Army'.

He became the engineer for the planning of a railway between Canal Street in the built-up part of New Orleans, along Naiades Avenue (now St. Charles) to Macarty's Point. The railway was to be the access to a planned development at that location, to be named Carrollton. The four-and-a-half mile railway, the New Orleans & Carrollton, was opened on September 25, 1835. Two locomotives were built for use on it by B. Hicks of Bolton, Lancashire. They were named the *Orleans* and the *Carrollton*.

Zimpel was appointed Deputy City Surveyor for New Orleans and as a practicing architect was also responsible for the design of a number of city buildings. Only one of his buildings, and that only in part – survives. This was built as Banks Arcade fronting on a whole block on Magazine Street. Four units at one end of this block remain in use as part of the St. James Hotel.

In 1834, Zimpel produced a multi-sheet map of New Orleans and vicinity, almost five feet square, which was engraved and printed in Germany. The top margin of this map has illustrations of a number of New Orleans' important buildings including several for which Zimpel had been the architect. It shows the line of the New Orleans & Carrollton Railroad, and the Magazine Street tramway route of this company that was not connected to the main line which are discussed elsewhere. Also shown is New Orleans' first railway, the Pontchartrain Railroad, which opened on April 23, 1831.

After being involved in the engineering for several other southern railways, ill health and the threat of malaria and yellow fever prompted Zimpel's return to Germany in 1837, where he continued to be involved in railway construction. As a result of his North American experience, he adopted American construction practice and used American-design rolling stock such as double-bogie passenger carriages. Locomotives were imported from Norris in Philadelphia and these served as models for engines constructed in Germany. He was the engineer for two railways, the line in Prussia between Berlin and Frankfurt am Oder, and the Hungarian Central Railway from Budapest to Bratislava.

In 1840, Zimpel had published at Vienna *Das Eisenbahnwesen von Nordamerika, England und Anderen Landen* … (Railway Practice in North America, England and Other Countries …) illustrated with 236 copper-engraved figures on 8 large folding plates. Among the illustrations is a double-bogie carriage with central entrances and top seats for the New Orleans & Carrollton Railroad that was built by M.P. & M.E. Green of Hoboken, New Jersey. Alas, there is not an illustration of one of the trams for local service in New Orleans. Charles Zimpel's career in railway engineering ended in 1843. Zimpel had strong religious inclinations and traveled to Biblical sites in the Middle East. In 1865 he had published in London a booklet proposing a *Railway Between the Mediterranean, the Dead Sea, and Damascus, by way of Jerusalem* … That route was used by the French-built Jaffa & Jerusalem Railway, opened in August, 1892.

In 1849, he was awarded the degree of Doctor of Philosophy at the University of Jena. He became a practitioner of homeopathic medicine, practicing in London for a time. He made major contributions in the field of homeopathy and published a number of books on the subject. Remedies formulated by Zimpel are still in production by Staufen-Pharma in Goppingen (Wurttemberg), Germany. Never married, he died at Pozzuoli, near Naples on June 26, 1879.

Portrait of Joseph Alphonse Loubat, 1799–1866 as a young man. Pastel by Paul Jourdy after Joseph Barthelmy Vieillevoye. (Collection of Mrs. Gerald Bland, New York City)

VI. Joseph Loubat and Europe's First Tramway

Alphonse Loubat, as he will henceforth be called, was born on June 15, 1799 at Saint Livraide, a town about 75 miles south east of Bordeaux, near the River Garonne. About 1826, he emigrated to the United States and set up as a merchant in the wine trade at New York. He imported vines from France and attempted to grow grapes for wine at New Utrecht on western Long Island, now part of the Borough of Brooklyn. In 1827 he published in New York a little book, with parallel English and French text, *The American Vine Dresser's Guide* to teach Americans how to cultivate grapes for wine production, and profit there from. In 1872, his son Joseph Florimond Loubat had the book reprinted with a steel-engraved frontispiece portrait of his father.

In 1829, Loubat married Susan Elizabeth Gaillard in New York. They had two children – the son Joseph

Florimond previously referred to, born in 1830, and a daughter Therese Aimee, born in 1833 who died in France at the age of 21, a year after her marriage. Loubat prospered in business and came to own considerable property in New York, and also in New Orleans and San Francisco. He erected a warehouse in 1841 on his property on Julia Street in New Orleans, for which a contract exists. It was replaced later in the 19th century by a larger building which is now the Louisiana Children's Museum.

As stated in his obituary in the *New York Times*, October 14, 1866, Alphonse Loubat retired from business in 1848 'with a competent fortune and returned to France ...' His trans-Atlantic activities continued. When in New York, his 'home away from home' was the Saint Nicholas Hotel on the West side of Broadway in the block between Spring and Broome Streets. He owned commercial property immediately south of the hotel, and on this property in 1878 his son Joseph Florimond had erected a cast-iron-fronted building that still exists at 503 to 511 Broadway.

Alphonse Loubat had to have been well aware of tramway developments in New York and New Orleans. In D. Kinnear Clark's *Tramways, Their Construction and Working* ..., London 1878 there is the following reference to the New York & Harlem Railroad with Clark's comments '... that it was unpopular, and was for a time suppressed [no evidence for this]. Tramways, nevertheless were revived in the same city [New York] about the year 1852 by the instrumentality of M. Loubat, a French engineer who recommended and laid down a tramway, consisting of rolled wrought-iron rails laid upon wooden sleepers ... 'I have found nothing to show that (a) Loubat was an engineer, or (b) he had any involvement with the building of tramways in New York.

In 1853, in the early years of the Second Empire of Napoleon III – at the time Baron Haussmann was transforming Paris into the city we know today – Alphonse Loubat made overtures to the city government of Paris for permission to build, at his own expense, an experimental tram line on the American plan (Chemin de Fer Americain). He received author-

ization to build a line along the Seine on the Avenue de la Reine, from the Place de la Concorde to the Barriere de Passy – a distance of about 2½ miles. It opened on November 21, 1853. The illustrations that were published of a ponderous top-seated vehicle that was used, in *L'Illustration* and the *Illustrated London News* bear no resemblance to the type of tramcar used in New York. I am reminded of photographs of vehicles of the Oystermouth Tramway at Swansea in Wales from the mid 19th century. It may relate to the tramcars/railway carriages of the New Orleans & Carrollton Railroad.

In fact, an illustration appeared in *Ballou's Pictorial Drawing Room Companion*, issue of September 8, 1855 of a scene purported to be in New Orleans showing a 'STREET RAILROAD CAR, NEW ORLEANS' which obviously derives from the illustration of Loubat's Paris tramway in the *Illustrated London News*! Quote the accompanying text, '... it is from a drawing made for us at New Orleans, by Mr. Bellew, and represents the horse-car in use on the city railroad. It is unlike anything used in north ...". Frank Bellew was born in India in 1828 of Irish and English parentage. His father was a captain in the British Army. He trained as an architect but became an illustrator. He emigrated to the United States about 1850. He is known to have supplied illustrations of American subjects to the *Illustrated London News*. In the case of the supposed illustration of a New Orleans 'street railroad car' it seems he cheated and used the image in the *I.L.N.* which was close enough!

Alphonse Loubat took out patents in France, No. 9169 of December 9, 1852, and 'Certificat d'Addition', August 8, 1854, plus an additional 'Certificat d'Addition' of November 22, 1854 in particular on the track construction, which was closely based on that used in New York – grooved rails similar in section to those of the Second and Eighth Avenue Railroads, laid on longitudinal 'sills' or stringers. The top corners of the stringers were chamfered to fit the underside of the rails which had corresponding fillets on each side, through which spikes secured the rails to the stringers. A British patent, 2789 of 1853 was also taken out on his track construction.

Loubat's tram line was extended beyond Passy to Sèvres in 1855, and to its western destination at Versailles in November, 1857. In 1856, the newly created 'Compagnie Generale des Omnibus' a consolidation of Paris omnibus lines, took over Loubat's operation and he sold his interest in the tram line to them.

The 'Compagnie Generale des Omnibus' developed a vehicle for use on their tramway operation which was almost more 'bus than tram. Larger than a 'bus, it had flanged wheels, but the front axle had a limited range of swiveling. These vehicles had top seats accessed by a quarter-turn stair on the rear platform. The driver sat at the roof level. Some of the earlier models had a side-entered first-class compartment at the front of the coach. The main compartment had side seats entered from the rear platform.

From 1854 to 1858, Alphonse Loubat served as the Mayor of Sèvres. About this time he had built a country house, 'Le Chateau des Bruyeres' at Sèvres. Gustave Eiffel purchased the mansion in 1892, and since 1953 it has been called 'Maison Eiffel'.

Alphonse Loubat died at Ville d'Avray on September 10, 1866. His widow, Susan Elizabeth [Suzanne Elisabeth] died in France in 1885. The son, Joseph Florimond, led the life of a dilettante and never married. He was a trans-Atlantic yachtsman among many interests. He wrote and privately published a *Numismatic History of the United States* in 1878. In 1893 Pope Leo XIII made him 'Duc de Loubat' in recognition of his generosity to the Church. Joseph Florimond was also generous to the Library of Columbia University in New York, and there is a plaque at the entrance to the rotunda of the Low Library in acknowledgement of Joseph Florimond Loubat as 'founder of the Loubat prize fund, and of the Gaillard-Loubat library endowment fund, 1892–1898'.

In the south ambulatory of St. Patrick's Cathedral on Fifth Avenue in New York there are two large stained-glass windows, one donated by Susan Elizabeth Gaillard Loubat in memory of her husband and daughter, and the other donated by Joseph Florimond. Joseph Florimond Loubat died in Paris on February 27, 1927. The Loubat's are buried in the family mausoleum in the cemetery at Passy.

Joseph Alphonse Loubat as an older man, frontispiece to *The American Vine Dresser's Guide*, an 1872 reprint of Loubat's 1827 book published in New York by C. Carwill. Reprint edition paid for by Joseph Florimond Loubat.

Tram of Alphonse Loubat's 'Chemin de Fer Americain' in the Cours-la-Reine. From *L'Illustration*, November 19, 1853. (Yale University Library, New Haven, Connecticut)

Alphonse Loubat's 'Railway upon the Road of the Champs Elysees, at Paris'. In the *Illustrated London News*, November 19, 1853. (Yale University Library, New Haven, Connecticut)

Apocryphal view of a tram in New Orleans in *Ballou's Pictorial, Drawing Room Companion*, September 1855. Drawing by Frank Bellew, a British-born artist who had worked for the Illustrated London News. Titled 'Street Railroad Car, New Orleans' it appears to be based on the above illustration from the *Illustrated London News* (Library of Congress, Washington D.C.)

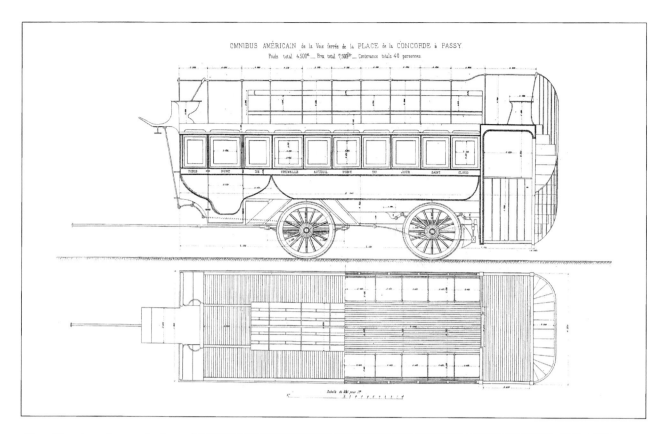

Above. Drawing of a tram built by the Compagnie Generale des Omnibus for the line, Concorde to Passy which was taken over from Alphonse Loubat in 1855 and extended to Versailles in 1857. In *Portfeuille Economique des Machines Relatifs a la Construction aux Chemins de Fer,* C.-A. Opperman, Paris, 1856. (Yale University Library, New Haven, Connecticut)

Right. Drawing of a tram built in 1856 for the isolated line, Rueil to Port Marly by the Ateliers of MM. Gustave Jean and Kellermann ... (*Etude sur les Chemins de Fer,* F. Serafon, Paris 1872)

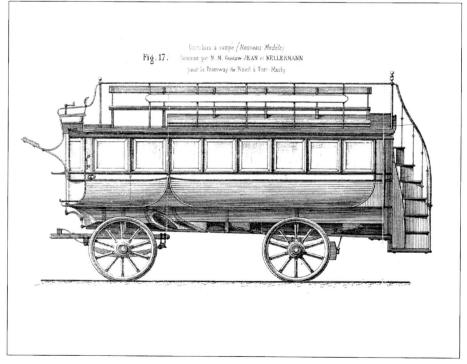

VII. The Builders of the First Tramcars

The mythology of the origin of the tramcar has it that the vehicles that John Stephenson supplied to the New York & Harlem Railroad in 1832 were the 'original street cars'. When John Stephenson was 'retired' about 1870 from the company he had founded – essentially for misuse of company funds, he took on the role of a spokesman and publicist for his company which had by that time become the largest manufacturer of tramcars in the World. Stephenson-built tramcars were being exported all over the globe.

This 'elder statesman' of the company took great pride in the fact that, almost forty years' earlier, he, personally, had built the 'original street car'. It can be said that these early vehicles, in their first use, had functioned as tramcars but they were designed to be railway carriages – to be drawn either by horses or steam locomotives.

Ultimately, through the 1830's and 1840's a vehicle that can truly be described as a tramcar evolved on the New York and Harlem Railroad and was in a fully-developed form when tramways started to proliferate in 1852. John Stephenson and his company had nothing to do with this evolutionary process – but who did?

About ten years ago, browsing the second edition of William H. Brown's *First Locomotives in America ...* (New York, 1874) in the chapter on 'Car Works', I came across the following:

'... In the early beginning of the street car introduction into our principal cities, that new branch of the business was added to the stage and carriage works, Sixth Street [Troy, New York], the firm of Eaton & Gilbert furnishing the new instrument of conveyance used in the city of Boston for many years after their introduction, and nearly monopolizing the patronage of the leading lines in New York City.'

William H. Brown (1808–1883) seems to be an improbable source of information about the actual builder of the earliest real tramcars. By profession he was an artist practicing 'scherensnitten' – the production of silhouettes in black paper. Many of those he produced of popular personalities were reproduced by lithography for sale. It just happened that as a young man he was present at the opening, on August 9, 1831, of the Mohawk & Hudson Railroad's line between Albany and Schenectady, New York. He sketched the inaugural train and produced a magnificent large silhouette portrayal of the locomotive *De Witt Clinton*, its tender and three passenger carriages – with engine driver, guards and passengers – all of which are portraits of the participants. The original, which is more than six feet long, is in the museum of the Connecticut Historical Society in Hartford to which it was given by its creator.

Forty years' later, he felt that, as he had been a participant in a major event of early American railway history, and in view of the inaccuracies that had appeared in print about that history, it was incumbent on him to correct the record. At the end of his book there is a chapter on an early producer of railway rolling stock – and in it his comments on Eaton, Gilbert's role in production of the first tramcars.

Eaton, Gilbert & Company

Orasmus Eaton established a carriage manufactory at Troy, New York in about 1820. In 1830 he was joined by Uri Gilbert as his partner and Eaton, Gilbert & Company was incorporated in 1844. The first railway carriages had been built by the firm in 1841. As has been mentioned elsewhere, Eaton, Gilbert had supplied carriages to the New York & Harlem Railroad and this lead additionally to the construction of specialized vehicles for that company's City line of cars.

As has been mentioned elsewhere, the appearance of Eaton, Gilbert trams is well documented in photographs. They were characterized by flattish arched roofs that extended over the platforms, and flat paneled sides. About 1860 the company issued a handsome catalogue of their products – from stage coaches to city omnibuses and trams, and their primary products, railway carriages and goods wagons.

The tramcar-building side of business seems to have diminished in the 1860's. Unfortunately, no order books are known to exist. The decline in tramcar building coincided with the rise of the John Stephenson Company. While no original Eaton, Gilbert trams are known to survive, there are preserved at Copiapo, Chile three tramlike vehicles that, if not built by Eaton, Gilbert were copies of that company's product. The cast-iron wheels of these cars were cast by Barnum, Richardson & Co. of Salisbury, Connecticut. This firm may also have cast the pedestals (trunnions) of the running gear.

By 1864, Orasmus Eaton had retired and the firm was reorganized as Gilbert, Bush & Company. In 1878, this firm built the first of 240 steam-hauled railway carriages for the lines of the New York Elevated Railway Company. The second of these built, No. 41 managed to survive as it was converted at an early date to a money collection car. Following electrification of the elevated railway lines in 1903 it was retained in this same function and given the letter G in place of its former number. Although not motorized, a control cab was installed at one end.

When the Third Avenue elevated line of New York City Transit was closed in 1955, several carriages that survived from the days of elevated railway steam operation were held back from being scrapped. G, and another slightly later passenger car which had been converted into an Instruction Car were donated to the Branford Electric Railway Association at East Haven, Connecticut, and transported on railway flat cars, then by lorry, to the museum's property in 1959. In 1983, the writer directed the restoration of G for display in New York, where for several days it was parked on the street in celebration of the opening of the 'Crystal Pavilion', a luxury building on Third Avenue. It was displayed some years ago at the New York City Transit Museum

in Brooklyn. I believe it to be the oldest surviving rapid transit car.

Eaton, Gilbert exported railway rolling stock to countries in Central and South America. None of their products seem to have gone to Europe, although a letter of February 25, 1847 exists from the company to an intermediary, offering to supply carriages and goods wagons to the Dutch government, giving prices, and specifying that they would be '... made so as to be taken apart & boxed and delivered at New York ...'.

However, Eaton, Gilbert might have been represented in England had George Francis Train had his way. Some years ago, a letter from Train to Eaton, Gilbert dated May 10, 1860 came to light. Train was seeking a supplier of trams for the line in Birkenhead: 'I wish you would send me the price of one of your cars – or still better if you would wish to put a car on the first European Horse Railway [what about Paris and others?] at Birkenhead ... This car I wish as a sample ... The gauge is 5 ft. 2 in. This may lead to important transactions if you can compete with the English makers ... The road will open in August. Please send me prints and information. Yours truly Geo Francis Train'. It is not known if Eaton, Gilbert responded to Train's request, but I suspect that he sent similar letters to the other American tramcar builders, Kimball & Gorton, Murphy & Allison in Philadelphia – and quite possibly to the Stephenson Company in New York.

No American built trams being available, it would seem, Train had to take recourse to a local carriage builder, Robert Main of Birkenhead to build the first trams for the line in that town. Train had with him models of the types of trams used in Philadelphia and New York, and that of the Philadelphia car was obviously the design chosen. Main did a creditable job, although some aspects – as one can see in surviving illustrations – are a bit 'clunky' compared to the prototypes.

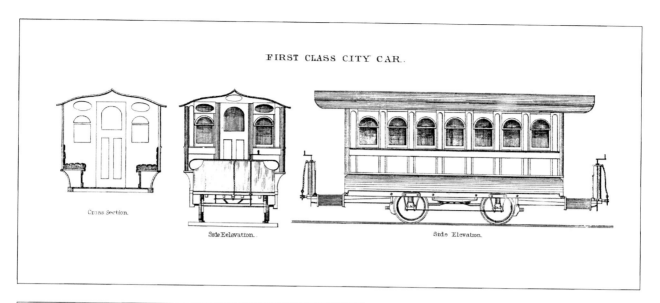

FIRST CLASS CITY CAR.

Cross Section.

Side Eelevation.

Side Elevation.

Top. End and side elevations and cross section of a tram, in a catalogue of the 'Troy Coach, Car and Omnibus Factory' of Eaton, Gilbert & Company, Troy, New York c.1859.

Above. Metropolitan Street Railroad, Boston, Massachusetts. Terminus of the line in front of the Granary Burying Ground. The Tremont Hotel is on the right. This line ran to the Norfolk House in Roxbury, Massachusetts. Wood engraving in *Ballou's Pictorial ...* December 13, 1856. (Yale University Library, New Haven, Connecticut)

Left. Tremont Street. Boston, Massachusetts. Tram in front of the Granary Burying Ground (at left) and the Tremont Hotel. 'Boston & Roxbury' on the letterboard of the tram.

Below. Harvard Square, Cambridge, Massachusetts c.1859. At the left is an Eaton, Gilbert tram of standard design. (Cambridge, Massachusetts Historical Commission)

Above. Harvard Square, Cambridge, Massachusetts c.1859 showing Eaton, Gilbert cars with variations of roof design. (Notman Photographic Collection, McGill University, Montreal, Quebec, Canada)

Left. Opening of the tram line in Santiago, Chile on June 10, 1858. An American engineer, Walter White Evans of New Rochelle, New York had worked on the New York & Harlem Railroad. He became involved in the construction of early railroads in Chile also the Santiago Tramway. The gauge of both the railways and the tramway was 5 feet 6 ins. Santiago's first trams were built by the Eaton, Gilbert Company of Troy, New York. (Allen Morrison collection)

Bottom left. A possible Eaton, Gilbert car – one of three preserved at a museum in Copiapo, Chile. The track guage is 4 feet 8½ins. (Allen Morrison photograph, 1991)

VIII. The Tramway/Street Railway Arrives

By 1852, twenty years after the inauguration of the New York & Harlem Railroad, New York had a population in excess of half a million – more than double what it had been in 1832. The northern limit of the built-up city in 1832 was not much north of Union Square (14th Street) but by 1852 the built-up city extended beyond 59th Street (the south end of Central Park).

New York's major avenues and streets were served by numerous omnibuses, but at best an omnibus offered cramped accommodation and a bumpy ride on the poor road surfaces then prevailing. Access, especially for ladies, was awkward as the floor of these vehicles was fairly high off the ground. The rear door and step was inconvenient to use and lacked proper hand-holds. The New York & Harlem's tramway between the City Hall and 27th Street had been a proving ground for tramway operation, and was also where the tramcar as a vehicle evolved to a state of practicality in the form of those constructed for the company by Eaton, Gilbert & Co. at Troy.

The stage was set for the first exploitation of tramways on a large scale. A tramcar, running on iron wheels (usually 30 inch diameter) upon iron rails offered passengers a much smoother ride than an omnibus, and offered less rolling resistance to the horses which pulled it. The body of a tramcar was much more spacious than that of an omnibus and easier to board and alight from as there were only two steps from the ground to the tram's platforms, and another low step from the platform into the saloon.

Tramcars were built in a variety of lengths in consideration of the type of service they were to be used for. The largest had a body length of 16 feet. The John Stephenson Company built bodies in two foot increments, from 10 feet (five windows) to 16 feet (eight windows). 10 foot and 12 foot body trams were light enough to be pulled by a single horse, on reasonably level ground. Many of the smaller cars were built single-ended – I believe the entire horse tram fleet in New Orleans was like this. Many, if not most of the

small trams were intended to be operated solely by the driver and if so, were equipped with built-in fareboxes into which passengers either directly deposited their fares, or in some instances indirectly by means of flattened, slotted tubes fastened to the inside of pillars and being set on a slant, had gravity feed to the farebox. The front bulkhead door of a single-end tram, or both doors of a double-end one were equipped with slides through which the driver could pass change when required. At each end of the tram was a lamp box with an oil lamp vented through the roof. This in many cases supplied the only light at night within a tram. A later option was additionally to provide one or more ceiling lights, the reflectors of which had numerous small mirrors to reflect the light.

Bells were attached to the undersides of the platform hoods, rung by leather ropes rove through eyes fastened at the centers of the roof ribs. In a one-man tram, passengers used the bell to signal the driver when they wished to get off. In a two-man car, the bells were additionally used by the conductor to signal the driver when to stop (one bell) and start (two bells). The driver used a crank-operated brake with his right hand to apply brake shoes to all four wheels.

The early tramcars, such as those built by Eaton, Gilbert; Kimball & Gorton; Murphy & Allison had window sash that raised. Stephenson, following omnibus practice, used a drop sash. Each side window opening was also equipped with a louvered blind. While trams with a drop sash were supplied by the Stephenson firm to the British market, at a fairly early date British tramcar builders chose to use fixed glass in the window openings, and this practice continued through the period of electric trams.

Track construction. The tracks laid for the New York & Harlem Railroad were set at the English track gauge of 4 feet, 8½ inches – the standard railway gauge. The first trackage that was run on, a single line between Union Square and Prince Street in New York, consisted of granite stringers, about 12 inches square in section laid flush with the road surface. A groove was cut in the stringers as a flangeway for the wheels, and strips of iron were fastened to the stone as a running surface for the treads of the wheels. This rigid construction – which was also used by other early American railways for urban trackage proved to be destructive to car bodies (See upper illustration on page 8, New York & Harlem track construction from Von Gerstner, *Die Innern Communicationen der Vereinigten Staaten von Nord Amerika ... Vienna, 1842–3*). In 1838, as noted elsewhere, a decision was made to replace the New York & Harlem's granite 'rails' as used in city streets with timber stringers to which flat-bottomed rolled iron of grooved section were attached. Timber stringer construction, but using flat iron rails had been used outside the built-up part of the city as the line was extended north of 14th Street. The stringers were kept in gauge by sleepers set at distances of five feet or so, and into which the stringers were notched.

A peculiarity of early tramway track construction – and which followed early railway practice as described in Von Gerstner's *Innern Communicationen in Amerika* was the use of flat rails on the outside of sharp (under fifty feet radius) curves. The inner rail of these curves was of a grooved section with a raised inside that acted as a check rail against the back of a wheel flange. The wheels on the outside of the curve rode on their flanges on top of the flat rails which in effect increased the wheel diameter relative to the inner wheel and thus assisted a car's movement around a curve.

While facing points were equipped with a movable point that could be shifted by the tram driver using a special iron bar (American 'switch iron'), trailing points were often without them.

Tramway openings. Two tramways opened for service in New York in 1852, the Sixth Avenue Railroad on August 11, and the Eighth Avenue Railroad on August 30. In 1853, two more lines opened: the Third Avenue Railroad on April 2, and the Second Avenue Railroad on July 17. The Third Avenue company shared trackage with the New York & Harlem on the Bowery.

Tramways opened in Brooklyn, across the East River from New York City, on July 3, 1854. Boston's first line opened on March 26, 1856, and Philadelphia's on August 1, 1858. By 1860, New York and Brooklyn had a combined total of 70 miles of horse tram lines; Boston had 56 miles and Philadelphia 90.

Boston is particularly rich in photographs of its early tramcars. There are also a number of good early views taken in Philadelphia and New York. A number of examples of these are included. An unusually good early view, found by Allen Morrison who has made an extensive study of the tramways of central and South America, is of the opening of the tramway in Santiago, Chile on June 10, 1858. The car shown is a standard product of the Eaton, Gilbert Company of Troy, New York.

Sixth Avenue Railroad cars and an omnibus in front of the 'Crystal Palace' on Sixth Avenue between (left) 42nd Street and (right) 41st Street in New York which is now Site of Bryant Park, behind the New York Public Library. Lithograph published by N. Currier, Nassau Street, New York 1853. (New York Public Library)

Right. Interior of a horsecar of the Sixth Avenue
Railroad. Wood engraving from *Harper's Weekly*, July 30,
1853. (Yale University Library, New Haven,
Connecticut)

Below. View in Sixth Avenue looking south-west,
showing the Jefferson Market. At the extreme left is an
omnibus. To its right is a Stephenson reversible-bodied
tram, and , to its right is an Eaton, Gilbert tram. Wood
engraving from *Ballou's Pictorial* ... October 17, 1857.
(Yale University Library, New Haven, Connecticut)

View looking north on
Broadway at the end (on the
right) of Park Row which was
the terminus of several tram
lines. This was the south end
of City Hall Park. Note theNew
York & Harlem Railroad tram
No. 33, 'Astor House & 27th
Street, Fourth Avenue'.
(New York Public Library)

Drawing of an Eaton, Gilbert
tram for the New York &
Harlem Railroad, lettering as
shown above. Plate 1 of *Aufsatze
Betreffend das Eisenbahwesen in
Nord-Amerika*. A. Bendel, Berlin,
1862. (Yale University Library,
New Haven, Connecticut)

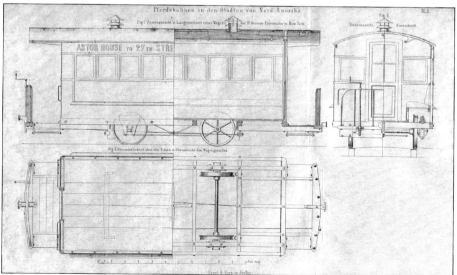

Park Row, looking south to Broadway. The church that closes this view is St. Paul's Chapel, built in 1766 – the oldest surviving building on Manhattan Island. The tram on the left is a Third Avenue Railroad car for Yorkville on the northern part of the island. The tram on the right is a New York & Harlem city line car just turned on to Centre Street. E. Anthony stereographic view, c.1859. (New York Public Library)

'Barn' of the Third Avenue Railroad Company on the east side of Third Avenue at 65th Street. (New York Historical Society)

IX. Kimball & Gorton's Philadelphia Car Works

This firm had its origins in New England with the firm of Kimball & Davenport in Cambridgeport, Massachusetts. Founded in 1832, it initially built a line of road vehicles, such as 'omnibuses, barouches, carryalls, chaises and buggies'. In 1834, railway carriages were added to the product line. An advert. for the firm has a picture of the factory, in front of which are lined up samples of production, including a four-wheeled railway carriage with a centre entrance. Manufacture of double-bogie carriages commenced at a fairly early date. Ebenezer Kimball died in 1839 at the age of 47, and was succeeded in the partnership by Alfred Bridges, the firm thereafter being called Davenport and Bridges.

In 1848, Richard Kimball, a son of the aforementioned Ebenezer, moved from Massachusetts to Pennsylvania, and went into partnership with Lorenzo Gorton. They had a factory built in Philadelphia specifically to produce railway carriages. After the introduction of tramways in Philadelphia, in 1857, Kimball & Gorton began the manufacture of tramcars at the Philadelphia Car Works. The model they first used was based on an Eaton, Gilbert design – variations of which were used on the existing tramways in New York, Brooklyn and Boston. A broadsheet advert. for the company of high-quality lithography shows at the top a typical Eaton, Gilbert style horse tram, and at the bottom a double-bogie railway carriage.

It would seem that Kimball & Gorton was desirous of modifying the Eaton, Gilbert design for the cars they produced, and a subsequent version of the lithographed advert. has the tramcar image replaced by an improved design. This featured an ogee-sectioned roof and shaped top lights for the windows of 'Gothic' influence fitted with ornamental glass. This attractive design saw wide acceptance, with the choice of alternative styles for the top lights. Many of the tram lines under construction at the end of the 1850's chose to have their cars built in Philadelphia by Kimball & Gorton (or Murphy & Allison – see later).

The Kimball & Gorton design, in the form of a model, was taken to England by George Francis Train,

to be copied in 1860 by Robert Main of Birkenhead for building the trams for Britain's first street tramway. Main also used this design in 1861 for trams he built for Australia's first tram line at Sydney, another scheme where Train was involved.

In 1861, when Train built his three trial London tramways in London, trams built by Kimball & Gorton (or possibly by Murphy & Allison?) were imported. When the municipal authorities in London forced the closure of the London lines – largely due to objections to the 'step rail' that Train chose to use, there remained in Britain a number of American-built tramcars. What happened to these almost-new tramcars? When the American, George Starbuck, an associate of George Francis Train, who served as manager of Train's London lines, established his tramcar factory in Birkenhead, the cars he initially produced were very definitely copies of the Philadelphia-model trams. Perhaps some of these vehicles were 'recycled' after their use in London? The ultimate fate of these first London cars has not yet been established.

Kimball & Gorton are shown in Philadelphia directories from 1851 to 1861. In 1862, Lorenzo Gorton is listed alone. The Philadelphia Car Works is shown thereafter to have been in the proprietorship of Joseph R. Bolton.

Murphy & Allison's Car Works

This firm had its origins in Philadelphia in the 1830s and at a fairly early stage of its history got into the building of railway carriages and goods wagons. Like Kimball & Gorton, it added tramcars to their products after Philadelphia built its first tram lines. An addition was made to their factory for this purpose. In 'Philadelphia and its Manufacturers' by Edwin T. Freedley, editions of 1859 and 1860, are the following comments on Murphy & Allison's manufacture of 'City Passenger Cars':

(The firm) '... directed their attention ... to the invention of improvements in Cars, a matter in which they have been peculiarly successful. One of the improvements noticeable in the cars of their construction is, *more head-room* by arching the roof, and making that portion which overhangs the platform dome-shaped, by which means the drivers and conductors are protected from the sun and the storms. They also place a lamp in the *center of the roof*, which diffuses the light more evenly and uniformly than the old plan; and other lamps in front of the overshoots, by which, on the one hand, passengers are furnished with a better light in ascending and descending the steps; and, on the other, the drivers have a better view of their horses … (T)his firm have already furnished seventy-five Cars for the Philadelphia Passenger Railways alone, while they have orders for nearly half as many more, besides some for Boston, Cincinnati, and other cities …'

The 'improvements' described are shown in Kimball & Gorton's revised lithographed advertisement, and it is possible that Murphy & Allison were the actual innovators of these details contributing to the Philadelphia design of tramcars. I do not know of any illustrated advertisements for this company, and it is not possible to determine the builders of the Philadelphia-style trams for which photographs exist. There are U. S. Patents issued to William C. Allison: No. 26,730 for 'Improvements in City-Railroad Cars', January 3, 1860, for lamps in a tram's 'overshoots' as mentioned in the Freedley article, and No. 28,530, 'City Railroad-Car',

May 29, 1860, for a system of installing top-seats on a tram by a structure that was wholly supported on the side walls of the tram, and which could be removed as a unit in the colder months.

Murphy & Allison's factory was destroyed by fire in 1863, in spite of it supposedly being of fireproof construction. An even more fireproof structure replaced it. After John Murphy died in 1866 the surviving partner created a new partnership with his sons as W. C. Allison & Sons. The firm ceased building railway carriages and tramcars in 1868, concentrating thereafter on the manufacture of goods wagons, etc.

In that year, John George Brill, a German immigrant who had worked for the firm for 25 years and had risen to the position of foreman of the tram building shop left Allison's employment and set up his own shop in Philadelphia. From this beginning and through the first third of the 20th century, the J. G. Brill Company became the World's largest builder of tramcars. It had absorbed many of its competitors, including the John Stephenson Company.

In 1859, the firm of **Poole & Hunt** in Baltimore built the first trams for the Baltimore City Passenger Railway, basically copies of the Philadelphia design. The body of one of these cars, No. 25 has survived, and is displayed at the Baltimore Streetcar Museum, and this would seem to be the oldest conventional tramcar to survive. In 1866, the firm of **Jackson & Sharp**, of Wilmington, Delaware built trams in the 'Philadelphia style' for the Easton and South Easton Passenger Railway in Pennsylvania, which is probably as late as the style was produced in the United States.

Trade advertisement of 1862 for Joseph R Bolton, successor to Kimball & Gorton.

Left. An early version of a lithographic advertisement sheet for Kimball & Gorton's 'Philadelphia R.R. Car Manufactory' showing an Eaton, Gilbert style tram. A reversed image of this car was used in Alexander Easton's book, *A Practical Treatise on Street or Horse-Power Railways,* Philadelphia, 1859. (Atwater Kent Museum, Philadelphia, Pennsylvania)

Below. The 'Philadelphia style' tram car developed by Kimball & Gorton c.1859. The advertisement above has been brought up-to-date. (Historical Society of Pennsylvania, Philadelphia)

Top. The Merchant's Exchange, Philadelphia c.1859, Third Street at Walnut Street. Note the variety of tramway rolling stock, including at the right a tram with top-seats. Also note the curved track in the foreground which uses a check rail on the inside of the curve against the back of the flanges. On the outside of the curve, the flanges rode on top of a flat rail. (Library Company of Philadelphia)

Above. Philadelphia tram at the Germantown Avenue and Gorgas Lane depot, 1876. Note heater under the middle of the tram's body. (Library Company of Philadelphia)

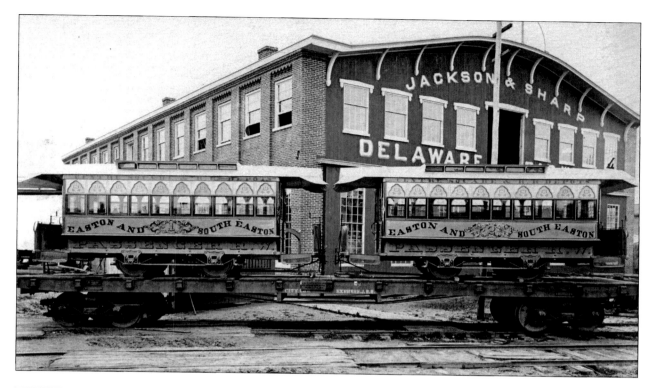

Top. Philadelphia-style trams built in the 1860's for a line in Easton, Pennsylvania by Jackson & Sharp's Delaware Car Works at Wilmington, Delaware. They are shown loaded on a flat-car in front of the Jackson & Sharp factory. (Delaware State Archives, Dover, Delaware)

Above. Philadelphia-style trams 104 and 139 built for Baltimore, Maryland c.1859 by Poole & Hunt of Baltimore. They are shown out of service and partly dismantled in a photograph taken in 1893. The body of a tram of the same type, No. 25, is preserved at the Baltimore Streetcar Museum. (Van Name collection, Library of Congress, Washington D.C.)

X. Alexander Easton

An important early contribution to the literature about tramways, and published in the period of the tramway's rise and development came off the press in Philadelphia in 1859. This is a small format, 149 page book, *A Practical Treatise on Street or Horse-Power Railways ...* Very little information has been found about its author, Alexander Easton. He stated (see the quote from the *Toronto Daily Globe* near the end of this section) that he was an Englishman.

In an attempt to discover more information about the man, the writer engaged the assistance of a genealogist, and from this source we have him been born in Colehill, Dorset, on the south coast of England, in April of 1828. In 1849 he emigrated to New York in the United States, his occupation given as 'gentleman'. In 1861 he is listed in the census for the County of York in Canada West (now Ontario, and in which Toronto is located) where he is shown as being married to a Chilean lady and of the Roman Catholic faith. He may be the Alexander Easton shown in the United States census for 1870, as living at 166 Fifth Avenue in New York with his Spanish wife, two young sons – one of whom was born in Canada in 1861, and two older women who were apparently servants. The New York directory for 1872 confirms the street address, with his occupation as contractor. There are problems with some of this information which needs to be verified.

Alexander Easton is listed in the Philadelphia directory for 1858, as a Civil Engineer and Lithographer. His home address is given as 627 North 13th Street, and his business address as 407 Walnut Street. Since he was a lithographer, it might be expected that he produced the plates for his book, but these were produced by William Boell whose business address is shown to be the same as Easton's. An enquiry to the American Society of Civil Engineers, founded in New York in 1852 had the response that the organization did not have a record of him as a member.

In addition to 116 pages of text in his book, there are 9 pages of advertisements including for Kimball & Gorton's Philadelphia Car Works, the Union Works of Poole & Hunt in Baltimore, Maryland – the builder of that city's first trams – and a full-page one for William Boell.

There are 24 lithographed plates, given Roman numerals of which I, II and XXIII are illustrations of tramcars. Plate I is a reversed image taken from a lithographed broadsheet advert. for Kimball & Gorton, and representing the early production of the firm based on an Eaton, Gilbert tram design. Plate II is an unusual single-end, top seat tram. It has twin quarter-turn stairs from the rear platform to narrow walkways cantilevered from the car sides above the windows. The top seats are shown protected by a striped canopy supported on iron stanchions. It also has the unusual feature of clasp brakes. There is no way to know if any trams of this design were actually built but it is reminiscent of the trams – probably built by Eaton, Gilbert – used in Valparaiso, Chile from 1863. The Valparaiso trams had round front ends, with the driver's seat at roof level whereas the illustration shows a conventional front platform with side steps. Plate XXIII is also of an unusual design, a form of roofed open tram with side entrances and side curtains for weather protection. This was designed by Easton for a proposed line between Camden and Haddonfield, New Jersey, but it is not known if any such cars were built.

Plates III and XXII are of track construction. The first of these displays a proposal of Eaton's to use wheels with outside flanges on step-rail track. The other shows the track structure adopted for use in Philadelphia, again with step-rails with track gauge of 5 feet, 2½ inches (which is still the Philadelphia tram track gauge). The rational for this gauge was that the flat surface of step-rails could be used by other road vehicles while a tram's wheels rode on the raised outer part.

Alexander Easton, with his Philadelphia involvement also used track gauges wider than standard 4' 8½" for some of the lines he engineered, such as that in Toronto, Canada where he used a gauge of 4' 10⅞". Toronto's extensive street tramway operation still uses Easton gauge. It has not been possible for me to identify other tramway lines Easton built, apart from those in Toronto, Montreal and Milwaukee, Wisconsin – this last dates from 1860, a year earlier than the other two. He may have been involved with a line in Buffalo, New York as the late Don Mueller advised me that a Kimball & Gorton horse tram in process of being delivered to the Eaton line in Milwaukee was diverted to Buffalo for display purposes.

Plates IV to XIX are full-sized rail sections, mostly grooved, as used in New York, Brooklyn and Boston. Plate X is rail used by the Eighth Avenue Railroad in New York, and XVII of Second Avenue rail. These are the obvious prototypes of the rail section patented by Alphonse Loubat in France. Plate XV is a form of step rail used in South Boston with a narrow (2 inch) 'tram' (flat surface). Conventional step-rails with 'trams' of 2½ and 3 inches as used in Philadelphia are illustrated on Plates XI and XII, and an improved version designed by Easton, with a very wide 'tram' is shown on what should have been numbered 'Plate XVI' (but has no Plate number on it) with a note, 'with 4 inch tramway for the accommodat'n of ordinary vehicles". George

Francis Train's British patent for Tramways included the Philadelphia step-rail design. Plate XIX, 'Proposed City Rail' is an early version of what was known as 'center-bearing rail'. A flat-bottomed version of it was widely used – I have a section of it from New York. This would seem to be the most objectionable section for use in a street, for its interference with other vehicles crossing the track.

Step-rail proved to be an anathema to British authorities and hastened the removal (if other excuses were not needed) of Train's London tram lines after a short trial. However it would seem that step-rails were the most widely-used rail section in North America. It persisted into the electric tram period as an optional form of girder rail, that is, optional to grooved girder rail. In the Village of Northport, on the north shore of Long Island in New York State, not far from where I am writing this, a single tram track running most of the length of the main business street survives, of this step-rail version of girder rail. Before the trams were taken

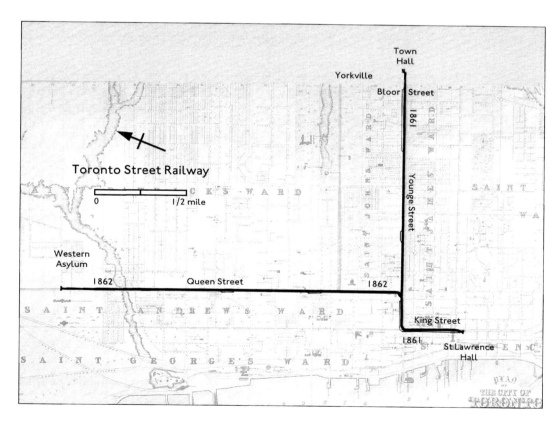

off in 1925, the street was paved in concrete and this, with the track embedded, is still in good condition.

Alexander Easton is known to me as the builder of the tramway in the City of Toronto, Ontario, Canada where I grew up and developed an interest in tramways. He also contemporaneously built a tramway in Montreal, Quebec (Montreal City Passenger Railway Company, opened November 27, 1861). The large tram system in Montreal was abandoned in 1959. Toronto is the only city in North America to retain conventional tramway operation on a grid pattern of streets. Much of this trackage follows that of the Toronto Street Railway, electrified in 1892 by the Toronto Railway Company.

The opening of the Toronto Street Railway's line was on September 10, 1861. It ran south on Yonge Street, from the Yorkville Town Hall (which also served as the tram depot) to King Street near the waterfront, and east on King to St. Lawrence Hall (still extant). The trams used were supplied by a Philadelphia builder – which one is not specified. The event was extensively reported by the *Toronto Daily Globe* (today's *Globe and Mail*).

Alexander Easton built the nearly three mile long line at his own expense. His negotiations with the City of Toronto were protracted over a lengthy period, and track construction commenced only three weeks before the opening! As a consequence, the track was in rough condition and some of the pointwork had not been completed. The photograph taken at the opening clearly shows the unfinished state of the roadway. and shows the lead car, with the Artillery band on its roof, decorated with flags. The four trams derailed frequently

on account of the track condition, but there were many willing hands to help re-rail them.

After the last car of the inaugural run had returned to Yorkville, a grand celebratory 'dejeuner' was held at 5:30 p.m. in the Town Hall. To quote the *Toronto Daily Globe* article:

'Mr. Easton stated that he had come among them a stranger about 11 months ago, his desire being to build here the pioneer street railway of Canada, after having pioneered works of that kind through the Western parts of the United States. He very much regretted that his business engagements had not permitted him to carry them on in his own native country. He had not been very much gratified when he had seen the press of England teeming with congratulations to an American [G. F. Train] for building street railways in England, while an Englishman was building the street railways of America (Cheers). He felt very sanguine, however, that he should build the street railways of England yet (Cheers) …'

Shortly after the Yonge Street line was opened, Easton built a second line, west on Queen Street, out to the Insane Asylum. Twelve trams were used for the two-line operation which was not expanded until the 1870's when more tracks were laid and additional trams purchased. The Yonge Street line lasted until 1954, when it was replaced by a subway. Trams still operate on King and Queen Streets.

Easton's design for a horse car to operate on the Camden & Haddonfield Railway in New Jersey. It is not known if any cars of this design were built.

CITY RAILWAY CAR

Lith. & Print. of W. Boell 311 Walnut St Phil.

Above. Top-seat tramcar designed by Alexander Easton. Similar cars to this design were built for Valparaiso, Chile in the 1860's by Eaton, Gilbert of Troy, New York. Frontispiece of Easton's *A Practical Treatise on Street or Horse-Power Railways …* Philadelphia, 1859.

Right. Three of the unusual single-end, top-seat trams of the Ferro Carril de Valparaiso, photographed by William Oliver in 1867. Their design, would seem to have been influenced by the above illustration. The driver sat on the roof, as in the early Paris tramway cars. The Valparaiso tramway was built by the British civil engineer Henry Gore in 1853. The track gauge was 5 feet, 6 ins. (Allen Morrison collection)

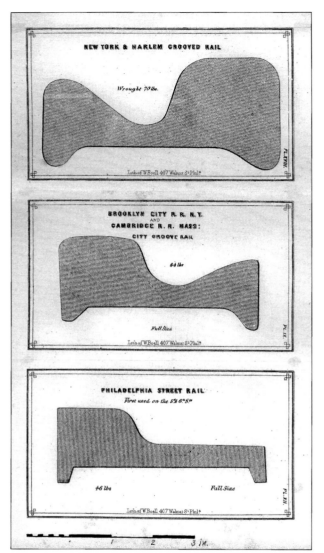

Left. Sections of street rails used in American cities, in Alexander Easton's *A Practical Treatise ...* Philadelphia, 1859.

Below. Typical North American track construction for tramways, using step rail, as illustrated in C. B. Fairchild's *Street Railways; Their Construction, Operation and Maintenance (Trams) A Practical Handbook for Street Railway Men.* New York, Street Railway Publishing Company, 1892. (John R. Stevens collection)

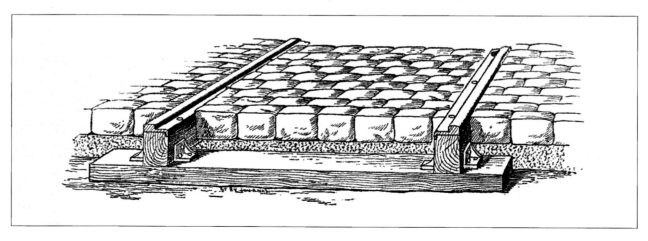

Opening of the Toronto Street Railway, September 11, 1861. At Yorkville Town Hall at the northern end of the line on Yonge Street. Note the band on the roof of the further tram. (Ontario Provincial Archives, Toronto, Ontario)

Philadelphia-type horse tram in front of the Yorkville Town Hall. Kimball & Gorton constructed the cars used at the opening of the Toronto Street Railway. (Rowley W. Murphy collection)

King Street East, Toronto, looking east from Yonge Street. The cupola
of St. Lawrence Hall can be seen in the distance. This was the southern
terminus of the Yonge Street line. c. 1860's. (Toronto Public Library)

PART TWO

Pioneers of Street Tramways in
the UK … and elsewhere

Alan W Brotchie

WORKS RELATIVE TO THE LIFE
OF GEORGE FRANCIS TRAIN

My Life in Many States and in Foreign Lands G F Train, 1902
The Nine Lives of Citizen Train Willis Thornton, 1948
Around the World with Citizen Train Allen Foster, 2002

Every last detail was carefully considered by Train, down to the
grey uniforms of the platform staff and even to their buttons, an
example of which is seen here. The uniforms were said by some
to resemble too closely those of Army rifle brigades.

Acknowledgements

Preparation of this second part of the work initiated by John Stevens has given an immense degree of satisfaction, and has brought together information, literally, from the furthest corners of the globe. George Francis Train's influence was felt, not just in the United Kingdom, where his patented style of street railway was used in six varied locations, and then in modified designs spread to the continent and Australia. Assistance has been rendered in the recounting of this by many individuals and institutions; including Ashley Birch, Brian Longworth, Adam Gordon, Alan Simpson, Ian Souter, and Brian Weedon of Melbourne.

George Francis Train, probably photographed shortly after his return to the United States of America, following his European tramway mis-adventures. The rosette in his jacket lapel may indicate that this was taken when he stood as a candidate for the Presidency of the USA in 1871/2.
(Washington State Historical Society)

On 16 January 1859 this 29 year old Boston born American citizen arrived in Liverpool, having as his remit to establish street railways or tramways in the 'Old Country'. It was recognised that improvements were needed (and possible) in urban street public transport. Here was the potential to make a lot of money, simply by importing the principles of street railways such as had been operating successfully in his country – and indeed in the city of his birth – for several years[1]. Three years before he had visited Paris where Alphonse Loubat's Chemin de Fer Americain – a line over two miles in length along the quai de Billy and the quai de la Conference – had operated successfully from 21 November 1853.[2] By referring specifically to its American antecedents Loubat clearly acknowledged that he was following a mode already commonplace in the United States of America.

Much of what has subsequently been written regarding Train has relied heavily on his personal promotional 'propaganda', and as a self publicist of note, he ensured that there was never any shortage of this. He proclaimed in almost every utterance relative to his British experiences that he had single-handedly introduced the street railway or tramway to Britain, and most columnists were happy to regurgitate the information as he provided it, more often than not forgetting that he was probably referring specifically to the improvements he had patented in the United Kingdom. Many subsequent writers on the subject have followed the same tack; even D Kinnear Clark in his 1870s opus states 'The modern tramway was intro-duced in England by Mr. G.F. Train ...'[3] and ignores the earlier inventiveness of his fellow countrymen. Here, wherever possible, reference has been made to original contemporary sources, treating Train's writings for what they became, particularly in his later years and in his autobiography, the selective recollections of an old man, plumbing the depths of his memory.

Train later frequently claimed for himself the distinction of having been the instigator of street tramways into England, but initially at least he appeared to intend to refer only to his patented improved street railway. The more generalised claim which gained wide circulation was however questioned within a decade of the event, with the authoritative journal *The Engineer* stating '... road and street tramways are generally supposed to have originated in so far as this country is concerned, with the notorious George Francis Train. This is not the case. Tramways were projected and in actual use, and successful, in this country long before Train's advent. From 1827 until 1839, when the railway was opened to Preston, a tramway was in constant use in that locality and which, in parts at least, had a grooved rail, that the stage coaches crossed daily at Bamber Bridge without accident or inconvenience.'[4] John Grantham, inventor of a steam powered tramcar wrote '... Mr George Francis Train, who has introduced nothing either novel or good ...'[5] was not wide of the mark. Charles E Lee, in his well researched 1953 paper[6] opens with '... his [Train's] work has often been accorded both priority and credit to which it is not entitled ...' Nevertheless, Train's self proclaimed prece-

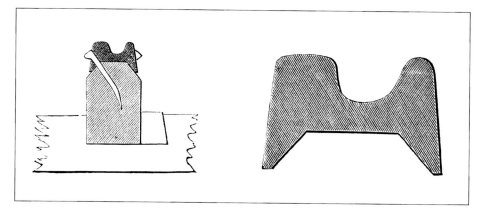

Detail of the 38 lb/yd rail used on the line laid in 1853 by M. Loûbat in Paris. It was found that the spiked fixings into the longitudinal sleeper below the rail soon loosened and that the track thus laid tended to spread in use. The illustrations of rail and track sections are from D Kinnear Clark's *'Tramways, their construction and working'*.

dence has ensured that it is he who, in virtually all references to introduction of street tramways to England, is given the credit – and to whom is also ascribed responsibility for the consequent failure of these first operations.

It seems more than likely that the development of street passenger tramways in Britain might have progressed naturally and perhaps with more success without Train's much vaunted contribution. Indeed if his derided step rail had not been utilised, growth might well have been more rapid and could have avoided the setbacks which his promotion of this patent style of rail brought, and appeared to damn the whole concept of street tramways in the eyes of many influential people.

In the United Kingdom, as had been already demonstrated in the USA, the boundary between railways (the earliest of which were horse drawn) and street tramways (which also initially depended on the horse for motive power) was exceedingly blurred. In America, street railroads were frequently continuations of inter-urban railroads, physically connected and often with freight workings through city streets. Many British tramways (earlier waggonways or tramroads) likewise obscured any attempt at a pure distinction. The Swansea and Mumbles line– the Oystermouth Railway – which received its Act of Authorisation in 1804,[7] was possibly the earliest of these, but there were others which fulfilled the criteria to be designated as passenger tramways. The Oystermouth is acknowledged as the world's first passenger carrying railway created under Parliamentary powers, with the date of 25 March 1807 reliably confirmed as the first operation of a timetabled passenger operation.[8] This line was later connected to the lines of the Swansea Improvements and Tramways Coy and also to the 'main line' railways, GWR and LNWR.

Even Scotland had, at this early date, three horse drawn passenger railways. The Elgin Railway in Fife operated a passenger coach between Dunfermline and Charlestown, inaugurated on 31 October 1833, and the 'Innocent Railway' from Edinburgh to Dalkeith commenced its time-tabled passenger service just a

week later, from 6 November 1833[9]. In the west, the Paisley and Renfrew Railway turned to horse traction after initial use of locomotives was found to be too costly. An amusing note of a journey on the latter line relates '… Returning from Loch Katrine on the day the *Australian* had grounded and stopped all the traffic of the Clyde … it was almost marvellous to find a huge and rude machine crowded inside and out, and with which, after the railway porters had once pushed it into motion, a single horse trotted off for three miles, apparently with much more ease than four horses would have drawn it on a common pavement'[10].

The city of Liverpool was well known to G F Train through his 1850 tenure there as office manager for his uncle's shipping enterprise Enoch Train & Co.[11] Following this venture he made his way to Australia, where he became partner in an independent shipping company which was highly successful during the 'gold-rush' period. Having made considerable initial profit, after he left Australia this enterprise eventually descended into insolvency in 1858.[12] His intervening years had not been spent idly, with (ad)ventures in – amongst other places – China, India, Egypt and Russia, before returning to the USA.

A passenger carrying horse powered tramway was already operational in Liverpool, Train's chosen locus for the initial application of his street railway. Successfully carrying passengers a 'tramway' had performed satisfactorily on the 'Line of Docks' railway from March 1859. A novel, patented, form of horse omnibus with flanges for its wheels which could be retracted and allow the vehicle to travel on roads which were not provided with rails ran successfully until after 1872.[13] There was later another more conventional passenger carrying street railway or tram line operated just beyond the Liverpool city boundary from Kensington to Old Swan for a short period after July 1861. It had been intended that this line would be extended to the city centre, but this never materialised.[14] [15]

Another person to beat Train 'to the draw' was W Bridges Adams, but he did not manage to translate his proposals into reality. His paper of February 1857[16] advocated the use of iron rails for street passenger carriage improved running, and stated his opinion that the only reason this had not been introduced to England by that time was "... the thing is so simple and easy, and the outlay needed so small, that there is no scope for either lawyers or engineers ...". Bridges Adams had been pursuing this course for several years, his first article, of about 1843 advocated rails in streets, flush with the road surface.[17] His ideas were to be found adopted in many cities, where a 'tramway' was formed by parallel tracks of (usually) granite slabs, with a dished running surface, benefiting horse drawn traffic, particularly on inclines. Examples of this system lasted in many industrial cities within recent memory, and only the general adoption of asphalt street surfacing saw their eventual demise.

In Glasgow there also existed a street tramway (used for goods traffic only) which pre-dated Train's patent. The 'Quayside Tramway' was laid with a unique iron rail with a dished groove. Plates 10 inch wide, with a formed groove in the centre, were provided for public use on several streets and quays, while narrower plates, 4 inches in width were laid where railway wagon use only was required.[18] This design facilitated the passage of carts, but could also be readily used by flange wheeled railway wagons; horse haulage only being used on these lines. It could have supported – but never did – a passenger service as operated in Liverpool.

It would appear that Train's interest in street railways crystallised in 1858, when a Philadelphia banker, Robert Morris, alerted him to the untapped potential in the United Kingdom, which then had considerable omnibus traffic in the major cities, but nothing by way of street railways. It can be fairly reasonably assumed that this was seen as a good target for investment with high potential for profit. It also seems probable that the Philadelphia Quaker establishment was behind the early financing of Train's exploits. Train returned eastward across the Atlantic on the steamer *Asia* [which docked at Liverpool on 16 January 1859[19]] in the company of the railway entrepreneur Joseph Nelson, who several years later wrote 'In December 1858 I met Mr Train at the Everett House, Union Square, New York. He was on his way to England on the business of the Atlantic and Great Western Railway, and I was returning from Canada on the business of the Halifax and Quebec Railway. In conversation I told him that I had just returned from a morning visit to a work in which I had been engaged seventeen years before – viz., the Harlem Tramways. This led to a conversation as to promoting the construction of tramways in England ... On the invitation of Mr Train I accompanied him on a visit to the late Mr James McHenry [another railway magnate] at Birkenhead, and on our way selected the route on which the first tramway in

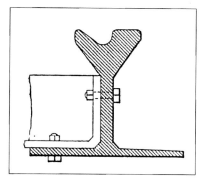

Rail profile patented by Charles Burn CE in October 1860, precursor of what became the conventional 'girder' rail. Had this had been utilised by G F Train, the development of street railways in the United Kingdom could have been entirely different.

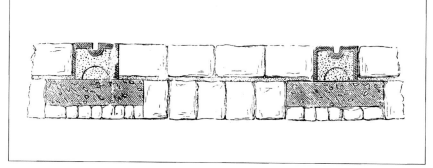

Glasgow Harbour tramway showing grooved plateway designed by Ransome, Deas and Napier.

England was built. I took an active part with him in nearly all the projected tramways, and visited many of the principal towns in the United Kingdom, but it was owing to the liberal financial assistance of the late Mr James McHenry that progress in the construction of tramways was made. The indiscreet charge brought by Mr Train against Sir John Shelley was fatal to our progress in London, and all the tramways for which only temporary permission to lay down had been given by the local authorities had to be taken up.'[20] Charles E Lee also indicates that another version of this relationship states that Train was employed in America by McHenry who introduced him to Morris, and that it was Morris who despatched Train to England, with a remit to obtain local authority agreements for tramway construction. He was to be assisted throughout by Mr Charles Hathaway to construct and Mr E Freeman Prentiss to manage, the various lines.[21] This chance meeting might have provided the catalyst for Train's (as always) extravagant efforts, on this occasion the object chosen being the establishment of street railways in England and beyond.

Train set to, in his words, '... the work of constructing street-railways in England ...' choosing Liverpool, the English city which he considered he knew best and where he felt he already had the necessary commercial contacts – or so he thought. His first approach to the Council appears to have been during the early part of February 1860 when he put forward his ideas for an extensive list of tramway routes. A line from the city centre to Garston was deemed most likely to be the first built. His application was pre-empted by one from locally established bus operators, made the previous month. To promote his cause he had printed a 56 page booklet[22], to which were appended the opinions of it from the local press – but naturally only those of a positive nature. One Scottish journal dismissed this early propaganda exercise 'The *brochure* is not written in the style most likely to commend it to sober-minded Englishmen and shrewd-minded Scotchmen. There is too much of rant and fustian in it – of that kind of writing that in America is admired as *eloquence*, but which on this side of the Atlantic is apt to be rudely designated as *bosh*'.[23]

Train's harangue was addressed to the Rt Hon Milner Gibson, MP, (President of the Board of Trade) and was deliberately directed towards rapid acceptance of Train's principles and for their application in the capital. At this stage Train appeared uncertain as to the type of rail intended to be used, as he indicates at the end of his work '... I have had manufactured two model cars with sleepers and rails, which show the principle in operation – one from Philadelphia, the other from New York – in order to give the style used in the respective cities, which will be on exhibition at the office of James Samuel Esq., C.E., 26, Great George-street, Westminster, London ... he [Train] is prepared, at his own expense, to lay down a rail in any street where the concession will be granted, in order to give an ocular proof of its public utility.'[24] The Philadelphia mode used step rails, flanged wheels on the cars, and was heavily endorsed by Train. The New York Third Avenue system on which the second model was based, was generally similar, but used a 'gutter' rail with a wide groove, and also used flanged wheels.[25] Train then went so far as to obtain a Patent for an 'improved' rail, and it must be that one of his main interests thereafter lay in the promotion of this. Indeed, on more than one occasion, much of the argument put forward by Train for his tramways was to the benefit which his rail conferred on all other road users. Much emphasis was placed on the advantage accrued by the 'improved' rail being flat, and thus having no groove in which stones could lodge.[26] Train claimed no monopoly for his vehicles on this track – merely the (forlorn?) hope that other road users would vacate the track when a tram was approaching. James Samuel CE acted as Train's consulting engineer (as indeed he had for the earlier tramway ideas for London based upon the Parisian line) on most of his tramway schemes, but even he was not entirely uncritical.

At this time Train's boundless energy saw him firing off in all directions, with tramway proposals created for many British urban areas from Aberdeen in the north, taking in Edinburgh and Glasgow, plus Newcastle, Manchester, Birmingham, Hull, Aldershot,

Portsmouth, Dublin, Cork etc, while also establishing what he entitled the American and European Tramway Company.

In many places Train's overtures were received positively, with a typical editorial – this from Birmingham – 'Will any of our readers be sceptical if we tell them that in twelve months from this time some of the principal streets in Birmingham will be traversed by railways, and that we shall be able to step into an elegant and commodious carriage at the bottom of New Street, and in ten minutes thereafter be landed at the Five Ways? ... the probabilities are all in favour of the belief that, in a very short space of time, Birmingham will have the honour of being one of the first English towns to adopt that swift, comfortable, and economical mode of street locomotion, so universal in America, the horse railway. Some time ago an enterprising Yankee, named Train, fit cognomen for such a speculator, introduced the idea of street railways to some of the municipalities of England. In common with every man who visits America, he had been struck with the swift, noiseless, comfortable, and cheap system of travelling in New York and other cities, compared with the rough, slow, comfortless, and inconvenient omnibus locomotion in England, and he has made proposals to the authorities of several towns for the introduction of this system ... it travels as smoothly as a Great Western train, and as rapidly as a pair of horses can cut along'.[27]

However Train was himself totally aware of historical precedents, and he was quite specific in a typically verbose lecture he delivered in Oxford on 5 July 1860 to the Mechanical Science Section of the British Association for the Advancement of Science, the annual meeting of the premier scientific body in a country which then led the world in such matters. His subject, not surprisingly, was 'Street Railways' and the benefits which adoption of such would bestow on such civilised countries as had not already seen the light: 'I cannot better appreciate your courtesy in permitting me to explain the merits of the street railway which I am now introducing to Birkenhead, to the distinguished *sarans* [sic] who have congregated at this meeting ... than by condensing into all possible brevity the substance of several lectures on this subject. The age of omnibuses in crowded cities has passed. The age of horse railways has commenced ... In the cities of Boston, New York, Philadelphia, Baltimore, St Louis and Cincinnati, the railway cars were displacing omnibuses in all the large streets. Like all practical labour-saving inventions, the people first oppose then advocate them. They have already become a public utility; and Americans would miss their railway-car as much as the English would their penny-postage system. The horse railway is a fixed fact. It has had a fair trial, and has met with striking success ... A century ago tramways were used in England ... Sir Benjamin Hall, if the short-hand notes taken at the interview between the City Commissioner and the Representatives of the London Tramway Company two years ago, are reliable, seems to have thrown cold water on the deputation, partly, to please his constituency, but mainly, because an accident happened to his carriage in passing some coal tramway in Wales ... That clumsy affair which Sir Benjamin alludes to in Paris has always been an eye-sore to the Emperor, and gives no better idea of the real Horse railway than does the *chemin de fer Americain* on the Neva's banks, at St. Petersburg, – the horse-power tramway from Carnarvon to Nantlle, or the Omnibus Railway along the docks in Liverpool.

The following are the advantages of the Street Railway:

1. Each railway car displaces two omnibuses and four horses ...
2. Wear and tear from these omnibuses being transferred to the rail, as well as that of many other vehicles that prefer the smooth surface of the iron to the uneven stone pavement, the rate-payers save in taxes
3. The Gas and Water Commissioners are not inconvenienced when making repairs, as the rails are laid on longitudinal sleepers which can be diverted in case of need; and as these cars, as well as the carts and carriages that take the rail, move on a direct

line, it is a self-constituted police system, saving confusion without expense to the public.

4. The cars move one-third faster than the omnibus, and so gentle is the motion that the passenger can read his journal without difficulty.

5. The rails are so constructed that no inconvenience arises at crossings from wrenching off carriage wheels, and as the improved rail is nearly flat, even with the surface, and some five inches wide, no grooves impede the general traffic, and the gauge admits all vehicles all vehicles that prefer the track to the pavement.

6. The facility of getting in and out at each end of the car and on each side, giving the passengers the choice of four places, together with the almost instantaneous stoppage by means of the patent brake, permits passengers to step in or out when in motion without danger, instanced by the fact that nearly seventy millions of passengers passed over the New York, Boston, and Philadelphia roads last year, with only twelve accidents …

7. In case of necessity, troops can be transported from one part of the city to another at ten miles an hour.

8. It is a special boon to the working man who, often in America, saves three-pence beer-money to buy a ticket from his work in the city to his cottage in the suburbs.

The advantages of this system are, that you ride in less time − with less confusion − less noise − less fear of accident − less mud and dust, and with the additional luxury of more regularity − more attention − more comfort − more room − better light − better ventilation, and with a greater facility of ingress and egress.

Birkenhead will have the credit of introducing the first Street Railway on this side of the Atlantic. My application was made in March, and on the 22nd of May the Commissioners affixed the seal to the contract, as arranged with my solicitors, Messrs Fletcher and Hull; the Ebbw Vale Company have agreed to deliver the iron in July; Messrs Crowe and Williams are preparing the timber; Mr R Main is at work on the carriages, to be ready in August; Mr Charles Burn, the contractor, will break ground the moment the material is at hand, under the engineership of Mr Samuel of London, and Mr Palles of Philadelphia, the resident

An 'artists impression' of his tramway vehicles at Marble Arch was prepared for Train to illustrate his 1860 Patent Application. It was subsequently also used as the frontispiece of the pamphlet directed to Thomas Milner Gibson, President of the Board of Trade, (whose residence was close to Marble Arch) that the street railway would not consist of trains of carriages hauled by steam locomotives. Train thereafter used versions of the image − sometimes in part only − to illustrate much of his promotional literature, envelopes, letterheads etc. (New York Public Library)

engineer; and in September Mr R Peniston, the secretary of the 'Birkenhead Street Railway Company (Limited),' will issue excursion tickets from Liverpool to Birkenhead Park and back for sixpence ... The system has succeeded in America: why should it fail in England?

The Lithograph of the Railway in operation at the Marble Arch, opposite the residence of the President of the Board of Trade, to whom I addressed my pamphlet on Street Railways, which I have had taken, may tend to remove the impression of the Irish Times, of a long line of carriages and a shrieking locomotive whirling through a crowded city ... the picture may explain better than the pamphlet; observation being quicker than reflection; the eyes satisfied the ears are content. [Train then goes on to relate his positive dealings with authorities in Liverpool, Manchester, Glasgow, Birmingham, Dublin and London.]

When I made up my mind last year to succeed in demonstrating the practicability of these railways in English cities, London was the starting point; but a practical Member of Parliament having assured me that most of the great undertakings were initiated in the provinces ... I applied to Birkenhead to shew them a pattern card of an invention ... all agreed it was a good thing ...' and so on for as long again, but deviating in his rhetoric from the thrust of the argument. He concluded '... if any member of the Association will do me the honour to attend the formal opening of the Birkenhead Street Railway on the 1st September next, I shall be most happy to see him and to welcome him to a collation worthy of the occasion.' If anybody present took advantage of this invitation they must have been sadly disappointed as the event referred to had taken place two days earlier![28]

Birkenhead

Liverpool's civic leaders were tardy in responding to Train's advances so, with the active encouragement of several of Merseyside's leading lights particularly Mr John Laird, attention was redirected across the river to Birkenhead. There the local authority, in the shape of the Birkenhead Improvement Commissioners' Road and Improvement Committee, received from Train a

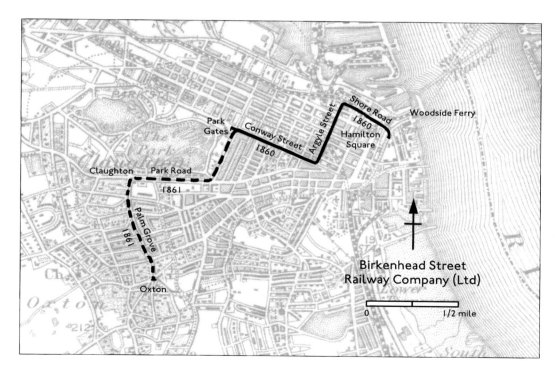

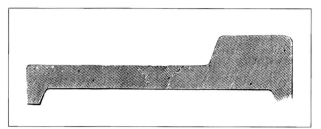

Train's 'Philadelphia' style step rail as laid at Birkenhead; rolled by the Ebbw Vale Ironworks it weighed 50 lb/yd.

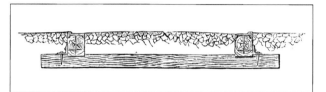

Section of the track as constructed for Train at Birkenhead in macadamised road. The original gauge was 5 ft 2½ ins, but this was reduced by 6 inches when his step rail was replaced by girder rails in 1864, to the standard 4 ft 8½ ins.

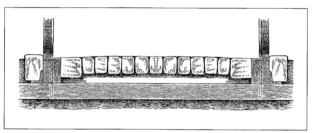

Train's rails as laid in a paved street, showing relationship with the flanged wheels of a typical tramway car.

letter dated 9 March 1860 setting out his proposals for horse railways '... into the leading thoroughfares of Birkenhead, as expressed in my letter to John Laird, Esq. of 21st February.' At this stage he envisaged a line from Woodside Ferry to Oxton and Claughton, out via Hamilton Street and back by Argyle Street, with a branch from Hamilton Square to Birkenhead Park.[29] This scheme followed the principle established in the USA of using where possible parallel streets for single tracks used by traffic in opposite directions. The planned centre for the rapidly growing town had been laid out initially in the 1830–1840 period by a Scottish architect, James Gillespie Graham, using as his inspira-

tion the style of Edinburgh's New Town. Hamilton Square to this day is very similar to the proportions and detailing of parts of Edinburgh – but the idea soon lost its impetus, with most surrounding streets becoming more reminiscent of what could be found over on the other side of the Mersey River in Liverpool. Birkenhead was then anxious to be seen in the vanguard of innovation and the American based idea of street railways was adopted with enthusiasm – not least by the Commissioner's surveyor Mr Mills.[30]

With John Laird's active backing, planning proceeded rapidly, with a Street Railway Committee formed, chaired conveniently by John Laird. Soon it emerged that the route had now been agreed as one of double track, from the Woodside Ferry (foot of Chester Street) along Shore Road, Argyle Street and Conway Street to the entrance to Birkenhead Park. This 125 acre pleasure garden, the town's pride and joy, opened in 1847, the first publicly funded such park in the United Kingdom, and formed the basis for the design of Central Park in New York.

This proposed 1¼ mile long route very soon (even before it was opened) prompted shopkeepers on Hamilton Street to petition for the return line to be laid along their street.[31] They were concerned that trade might pass them by! Permission for this was given at the beginning of August.[32] It was also a major selling point to other frontagers, that the value of property along the line would rise, following American precedents, after completion of the line. A petition was also presented that the line should extend to Oxton and Claughton, but wise counsel prevailed, suggesting that the first line should be given a proper trial before extensions were contemplated. Work started in earnest on 10 July 1860, excavation for the track commencing at the Park entrance with rails strung out along the length of the route.[33] These, to Train's Patent were supplied by the Ebbw Vale Ironworks in Wales, and work was started as soon as they were to hand. The contractor was named as Charles Burn, although Charles Hathaway later claimed to have been the contractor for all six of Train's lines. Construction of four cars (initially only three were intended) was entrusted to the established local coach-builder Robert Main, and progress was sufficiently advanced to allow Andrew Palles – the American resident engineer supervising the work on Train's behalf – to take the first car out on the line at 4.00 am on 22 August.[34] A run was made over the entire route on Monday 27th with several of the directors of the company aboard. Construction may have – in theory, at least – been undertaken by the 'American and European Tramway Company' for which Train was said to be the agent and Palles their local engineer.[35]

A Joint Stock company with capital of £10,000 in £10 shares [equivalent to c£8 million in 2014] was created to finance the line; with among the directors Samuel George Taylor (later Chairman of the company), Charles Moore, Samuel Cearns and John Alfred Marsh named. The company secretary was Richard Peniston with the registered office located in Liverpool, at 23 Lord Street. From the capital it was later said, when Train sold his personal holding of £600, that he had also received a douceat [sic] of £5,000[36] – it is considered that the most likely interpretation of this is as 'douceur' – a 'present, bribe, or sweetener'.[37] It is also said that Train held five hundred of the original shares.[38] However that lay in the future as Birkenhead braced itself for the formal opening of

This print of Birkenhead car number 2 is probably taken from the original plate negative, and because of its historical significance has been much reproduced. It was recorded in the centre of Birkenhead, in Hamilton Square. Train is on the top deck, at the left hand end, possibly the only man present without a hat! Immediately below him at the corner post of the tramcar is Robert Main, the local coachbuilder who built the first four Birkenhead tramcars. On the extreme right end of the top deck, the youth is twelve-year old James Clifton Robinson whose subsequent career in transport culminated in his position as Managing Director of London United Tramways. He was knighted in 1905.

Of the four initial cars supplied for the inauguration of the short Birkenhead line, two were double deck, and two were single deck intended for winter use. This is one of the latter cars in an engraving made from a photograph which seems subsequently to have been lost. The scene is at the junction of Argyle Street and Cleveland Street, and was probably taken on the same occasion as the preceding view, on 30 August 1860. Train stands closest to the camera on the platform, with Main at the horses' heads. From Birkenhead Corporation's brochure of 1951.

Train's tram, to which grand event he had issued one thousand invitations, of whom (perhaps fortunately) only about one third actually turned up.

The four new 'omnibuses' or tramcars, made an appearance at ten in the morning and were immediately put into public service, until about 1.30 pm when they assembled at Woodside to meet the invited guests. With a band playing on the first, the cars made their way to the Park, then returned the participants to the 'sumptuous and liberal *dejeuner*'. This was laid out within a marquee set up within Robert Main's newly-built coach building workshop in Canning Street just off Argyle Street, which also initially doubled as the depot.[39] Despite inviting all the crowned heads of Europe, including Queen Victoria and Prince Albert (but excluding only the King of Naples, since Train had thought that Garibaldi would have supplanted him by then) none was able to attend. After doing justice to the repast Train took the chair and was obviously in his element; numerous toasts were made and responded to, and it is noteworthy that in responding to the toast to the Birkenhead Commissioners John Laird said '... One gentleman had stated that the line would not answer, and that it would be destructive to his omnibuses, but he [Mr Laird] was glad to see that that very gentleman had shown his good sense by driving the first new omnibus to the Park. That showed that people should not find fault with a new scheme until it was tried ...' Following at least twelve such toasts the long detailed report of the event ended; 'Two or three songs followed, and the proceedings, which abounded with good feeling and hilarity, were then brought to a close'. Train knew how to throw a good party; tee-total himself, he ensured his guests were properly catered for, 'the wines were abundant and excellent'[40]. Laird's comments could be interpreted to indicate that a vociferous opponent of the tramway – and local omnibus proprietor – James Evans assisted at the opening; but he also soon lodged complaints against the tramway for damage to wheels of his vehicles. On the first day, 30th August, some 4360 passengers were carried on the tramway between noon and 7 pm. The cars were predominantly pale green and drivers and conductors were smartly turned out in suits of Oxford grey, 'very much in the appearance of Volunteer riflemen'.[41]

Considerable detail of Birkenhead horse–car operation is contained elsewhere, which does not require repetition here.[42] Scrutiny of contemporary writings can, however, add further information. It has been stated that the four vehicles provided on the opening day were manufactured locally utilising parts shipped from the USA.[43] However, if parts could be got from the other side of the Atlantic, why not complete trams just as promptly? Robert Main of Birkenhead is given full credit on every occasion Train or the contemporary press refers to the manufacture of the vehicles, and indeed when, some five months later, a car was imported from the USA, much was then made in the local press of its qualities 'They have just introduced a very light and elegant car from New York, in which we would advise our friends to take a ride to Birkenhead Park'.[44] The order to Main had been given immediately after the Birkenhead Commissioners signed the contract (on 22 May) with delivery required in August;[45] in fact the first car was noted on the rails before the end of that month, a trial run taking place early in the morning of 22 August. Design of the vehicles is stated as having been by Palles, employed under Mr Samuel. Palles had good relevant knowledge,

Advertisement from the *Liverpool Daily Post*, 28 August 1860.

Advertisement from the *Liverpool Mercury*, 30 August 1860.

Invitation to the inauguration banquet on 30 August 1860. Despite being for an event held in Birkenhead, the Marble Arch scene is used as the centre-piece.

having been involved in construction of street railways in Philadelphia, where, he said, considerably more opposition had been experienced than at Birkenhead.[46] Not long after the opening of the tramway Palles gave a lecture to the Liverpool Polytechnic Society during which he told the enthralled audience that on one occasion a car at Birkenhead had carried 116 passengers![47]

Train's principal object was to have his street railway philosophy adopted in the capital city, hence Birkenhead was looked upon by him very much as a demonstration line, not really serving an important role in transporting the population of the Merseyside township, but there to show practically the principles and benefits to other interested parties. Deputations from such places were frequent visitors. As early as September, Edinburgh's Roads Board was approached by Train, and a letter appeared in the columns of the *Scotsman*[48] from William Miller, a member of the Edinburgh Stock Exchange, who was on the invitation list for the Birkenhead opening, extolling the benefits of tramways and advocating their introduction to Scotland's capital city. Obviously in this instance Train's generous hospitality had not gone unrewarded.

Miller said that he had spent several hours in minutely inspecting the railway and carriages along with Mr Pallas [sic] the engineer who superintended the construction of the line, and that '…an eminent engineer intimately acquainted with Edinburgh did not know of any city better adapted for these railways than our own, and more especially between Edinburgh and Leith. I saw one of the company's carriages drawn easily by two horses; it was quite full of passengers, and was seated for 24 inside, with room for other 8 or 12 to stand in the centre, and about 5 at each end, besides 24 seated outside – in all between 60 and 70 …'. Edinburgh's City Paving Board was favourably disposed relative to a line between the West End of Princes Street and Leith which included a return line by York Place, Queen Street and Castle Street. Train's terms were identical to those he offered generally; that he would do everything to satisfy the relevant authorities and remove the line at no cost, etc. A letter[49] from

Liverpool's Mr Newlands, engineer to the Board of Public Works advised 'Every day's experience at Birkenhead proves that these railways are great conveniences for the people, the general public – but there is as little doubt that much profane swearing is evoked by them from the upper ten thousand who drive or are driven in their own vehicles.' The 'powers that be' in Edinburgh decided to wait and see how things developed … a not unusual decision for that city. However others considered that Edinburgh was totally unsuited for street railways, 'If there is a city in the world for which they are not adapted, it is Edinburgh, with its streets not broader than to afford room to ordinary traffic, and its numerous steep inclines'.[50]

A Glaswegian participant in the Birkenhead opening was less sanguine. 'Immediately on landing at Birkenhead this forenoon, I met a large crowd earnestly engaged inspecting and criticising what Mr Train terms a railway car, but what in Glasgow would be called a 'bus, painted in gaudy colours, and reflecting great credit on the taste of the artist, but not nearly so substantial in any respect as our Partick and many of our city 'buses. The car stands much lower than our 'buses, thereby making it much easier to get off and on; and when once inside there is an air of comfort about it which I hope they may long retain … The guage [sic] is 5 feet 2 inches, being 5½ inches broader than the railway guage; the plates are laid along the principal streets … I send you the programme. From the remarks printed on the back of it you will be able to form some idea of the entertainment. The viands, wines and speeches were of the kind A1; and I do not remember having spent a merrier two hours … But, to come to the practical conclusions, and enquire whether or not the thing will succeed. I really very much doubt it until Mr Train makes very material alterations in his plans. From what I saw I firmly believe it took more power to draw the car along the rails than what it takes to draw our 'buses along the streets. With an ordinary full load, going up a slight incline with three horses, it actually stuck fast, and had to be pushed up by the folks outside. There was also some very disagreeable joltings, which, by a little ordinary care and attention in the construction, could easily have been avoided. But to call this street railway a patent, and the first of kind on this side of the Atlantic, is one of those *sells* which occasionally come over. Why, in our very midst, as far back as I can remember, we have had in the Dalmarnock Road, a much more suitable and better street railway than Mr Train's. It has all the advantages of his, and a great many more which his has not got – such as being able, when wanting to let a 'bus or cart pass, to go off the rail, and then quietly to go on again. I have often thought that it would very much have assisted our traffic if these rails had been carried right on from the east to the west of our principal streets. I hope, if our authorities are really in earnest about assisting the traffic, they will adopt something more workable than Mr Train's street railway.'[51] A least here was one correspondent who was prepared to depart from the 'blurb' produced by Train for regurgitation by the topical press.

During the first week of November 1860, after only two months of operation, permission was requested from the Commissioners for several new lines and some adjustments to the existing layout, particularly at the Ferry terminal;

   i. A single line up Claughton Road to Park Grove by Water Street and across Mr Ravenscroft's field to Claughton Road
   ii. A connection along Park Road East
  iii. A connection along Bridge Street between Hamilton Street and Argyle Street
  iv. A siding into Church Street and one in Chester Street.

It was also decided that the existing rails from the foot of Chester Street to the start of Shore Road should be removed, hence it appears unlikely that the final element above was pursued, although the Church Street siding was approved at the Commissioners' meeting at the end of November. That same meeting gave authority for a single line from the Park Entrance along Park Roads East and South as far as Palm Grove, also the Bridge Street connection, but required that one of the tracks in Conway Street be removed.[52] A tacit acknowledgement of problems experienced was made in the statement that for the new lines the rail upstand would be reduced from 7/8 of an inch to ½ inch. To fund the additional works the capital of the company was increased to £17,650. It was also noted that in the first four weeks of operation no less than 57,716 passengers had been carried.[53]

Operation was not without problems, which may have centred on poor performance of the locally cast wheels during the first winter of operation. In January 1861 Train wrote 'I am importing from Philadelphia, for the use of my street railway carriages, wheels which are not affected by frost and which can not be broken

Charming contemporary drawing of a two-horse open car proposed by Prentiss for the Birkenhead tramway. Obviously looking to the tourist trade, for whom a tram journey to Birkenhead's new magnificent Park was a real day out, it never appears to have progressed beyond this stage. The seats are supported by the trusses for which Prentiss was granted UK Patent 2619 of October 1860, designed so that the support of these (normally top deck seats) was carried by the sides of the car, rather than the roof. (© National Tramway Museum)

by any ordinary concussion. These wheels would remove one cause of many recent disasters ..."[54] The disasters to which Train referred were probably on main line railways, and indicate the serious consequences of wheel defects in low temperatures, and that he sought to reassure the public that the matter could, and would, be resolved speedily.

While Train was no longer directly involved in his pioneer Birkenhead line, the legacy of his early dealings cast a long shadow over the tramway. The town's civic leaders almost without exception now considered that the tram represented a valuable – and progressive, up to date (even if American) – asset to the new town, while many positively minded citizens appreciated the benefits which the new transport system provided above and beyond that given by Evans' and Gough's rattling buses. While this study is concerned in general terms with Train and his sometimes malign influences, it is only proper that relevant subsequent events in Birkenhead be considered before turning attention to his activities elsewhere.

Extensions were approved at the beginning of May 1861, with Mr Harrison of the Commissioners' Street Railway Committee recording '... all the objections that had been raised to the street railway system had vanished completely; and all the miserable predictions about the ill consequences it would cause had utterly failed".[55] The company resisted pressure to extend simultaneously to Oxton and to Claughton – only at the latter locus was there land owned by the Commissioners, who in wishing to develop it, saw benefits from a tramway extension. The company did not concur, building the Oxton line only, which probably opened during August.

Robert Main may have developed a 'chip on his shoulder' with regard to Train's activities, in particular the decision to have subsequent cars constructed elsewhere. In July 1861 Main petitioned Birkenhead Commissioners regarding the dangers, as he perceived them, of Train's rails, proposing that the omnibuses used on the road 'should be so constructed as to move off and on the line when the rule of the road or the public convenience should demand it ...'[56] As he had not

long since patented a design of wheel which would permit just this, his position was perhaps not entirely to be wondered at.

At the beginning of October 1861, E F Prentiss, now employed as general manager of the line, approached the Wallasey Local Board with a proposal for an extension of the line from the existing tramway, by way of Seacombe and Egremont to New Brighton, with an extension south to serve the railway station at Monks Ferry.[57] However the next Board meeting decided that this was 'not expedient at the present time'.[58]

In early 1862, Thomas Evans, a Birkenhead bus proprietor, and one of the town's Commissioners, and who had obviously lost patronage to the street railway, decided that he would test Train's statement that the rails were available for anybody to use. He had two new vehicles built by Main '... for the purpose ...'[59] and put them on the rails from 30th January. His point was probably to cause as much disruption as possible, rather than to operate a viable alternative service, and to this end he certainly succeeded. However at that time he made the statement '... it was impossible ... for his two carriages to block up nine belonging to the company.' Considerable interference was caused to operation of the street railway and to other road traffic by the impasse, with matters taken to the local Magistrates Court on 7 February. Here blame was attached unequivocally to the drivers of company cars number 3 (John Hughes) and 4 (George Davies) who were said to be acting on instruction of their masters. Fines of up to 40 shillings were imposed – then a considerable amount.[60] The Birkenhead dispute was resolved when the directors of the Street Railway Company agreed that Evans should take over working of their line and remove his competing cars.[61] This took effect from Monday 10 March.[62]

A dispute with William Jackson MP, a major landowner in the area, resulted in the company being landed with a fine of £200 at Chester Assizes, the direct consequence of which was a cessation of operation from [probably] 5 August 1862 until resumed – but with a different lessee – thirteen days later, as a consequence of a public petition bearing a large number of signatures. It was reported that '*Young America*' had recommenced running between the Ferry and the Park, and shortly afterwards that the lessee was now Charles Castles of Liverpool.[63] After persevering with him for about two years the company took operations into their own hands.

Mr Harrison's earlier statements were to be questioned, however, at an Extraordinary General meeting called for the end of December 1863 to agree proposals for alteration of the line by completely re-laying the track with grooved, rail and at the same time reducing the gauge from 5 ft 2½ ins to 4 ft 8½ ins. This followed after the similar alteration successfully undertaken to the Train-patent tramway in the Potteries (qv). To supervise the Birkenhead work an American civil engineer, Thomas Wiswell was recruited and who was subsequently engaged to manage the line. In March 1864 he showed the Commissioners a sample of the new design of rail.[64]

This major re-construction was soon started; not content with replacing Train's discredited rail, the proprietors of the streets traversed (and those not so blessed) demanded a reorganisation of the layout of the lines. Work started in earnest at the Ferry on 25 July 1864, with the system worked as two sections; one part (reducing daily) with the old rails to the old gauge, the other (increasing daily) to the new gauge with new rails. Permission was granted for a siding on to waste ground off Vittoria Street to store the trams temporarily. The new construction provided essentially an entirely new tramway; a new single track was laid on Price Street and Vittoria Street for outward traffic to the Park, while Conway Street and Hamilton Street became the route for inbound traffic. [Vittoria Street is rendered as Victoria Street in some contemporary references] At the Ferry a new terminus, built on a new private approach carriageway provided by the Ferry Commissioners came into use on 21 November 1864.

The company was never a financial success in its early years. When Wiswell was speaking before the House of Commons Committee debating the bill of the Metropolitan Street Tramways in April 1869, he acknowledged that the forty or so shareholders had never received a single dividend, and that an actual loss of £1896.11s10d had been incurred in 1867, but that in the last year revenue of £5600 had to be set against expenses of £5000, so perhaps better times were just around the corner.[65] The pioneering role of Train's first tramway has never been knowingly under-sold, especially by that gentleman himself. It survived many tribulations, but paved the way for many subsequent profitable similar enterprises, and was the first of a continuous succession of development and improvement which has led to efficient light rail transport in many cities in the British Isles.

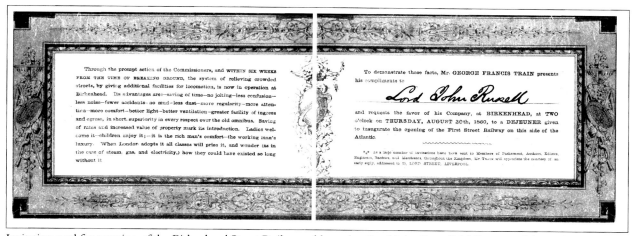

Invitation card for opening of the Birkenhead Street Railway, addressed to Lord John Russell M.P., a son of the Duke of Bedford. He later became the last Whig prime minister of Britain.

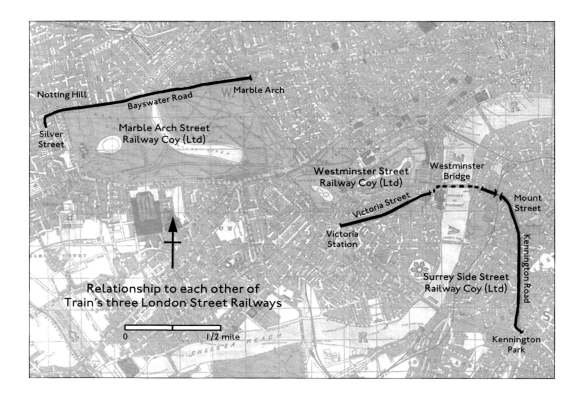

Notting Hill
Marble Arch
Bayswater Road
Silver Street
Marble Arch Street
Railway Coy (Ltd)
Westminster Street
Railway Coy (Ltd)
Westminster Bridge
Victoria Street
Mount Street
Victoria Station
Kennington Road
Surrey Side Street
Railway Coy (Ltd)

**Relationship to each other of
Train's three London Street Railways**

0   1/2 mile

Kennington Park

London

It has been recorded that as early as 1850 a proposal was made to lay a tramway from Piccadilly to the Great Exhibition at Hyde Park by Thomas Wright of 9 George Yard Lombard Street. Wright had models of his patented style of rails, wheels and omnibuses for use thereon – plus 'working samples ready for use at a moment's notice'. It was stated that this could have been in operation by 1st May 1851.[66] During September 1853 several newspaper correspondents suggested introduction of the '… Paris plan of a monster omnibus by rails … similar, but on a more comprehensive scale than that proposed for London … two years ago …'[67] Alphonse Loubat imported the principle of the American street railway to the French capital, with a line opened on 21 November 1853, so these thoughts preceded the opening of Loubat's line.

These proposals appear to lie dormant until 1857 when a Mr W Bridges Adams read a paper to the Society of Arts on the 'Application of rails for horse traffic in the streets and environs of London'. He referred to lines already operating in America and Paris and recommended a network of 70 miles from various central points to the suburbs, using vehicles carrying fifty-six passengers.[68] This seed fell on fertile ground and October 13 1857 saw incorporation of the London Omnibus Tramway Company.

The tone for subsequent events was set, when on 18 February 1858 a deputation from the promoters of the London Omnibus Tramway Company's Bill waited upon Sir Benjamin Hall, 'to try to enlist his support to their bill for constructing tramways for a new species of omnibus through certain thoroughfares of the metropolis. After listening to the deputation, Sir Benjamin replied that he had maturely considered the plan, and of all the monstrous propositions which had ever been made or presented to parliament this was the worst. It was utterly impossible that these trams could be laid on Macadamised roads, for instance. He ridiculed the idea of setting up the tramways in the Champs Elysees or in New York as an example, as they bore no analogy to the thoroughfares of the metropolis. Every parish through which the line passed was petitioning against the bill, and his advice to the promoters was that they should withdraw it at once. The deputation then withdrew.[69] Hall added that he would give the Bill his most determined opposition, and when the Bill was presented for its second reading he tabled an amendment which ensured that it proceeded no further.[70] Sir Benjamin Hall (First Baron Llanover after 1859) was a Whig MP for (initially) Monmouth then Marylebone, who had trained as a civil engineer. It is understood that his intense antagonism arose from his carriage having had its wheels damaged when crossing a colliery tramway in his constituency.

Hall was not without his critics, and his autocratic attitudes ruffled many feathers, '... his vanity induces him to oppose every improvement that he cannot pretend to have originated ...' was just one such example. The writer, much in favour of the proposal, indicated that for twenty-five years [a slight exaggeration] New York had benefited from just the type of street conveyance which Sir Benjamin condemned out of hand.[71]

'It is utterly impossible that the iron rails or plates upon which the carriages were to run could be laid on macadamised roads, for instance, with a certainty of always being kept on precisely the same level as the road; and carriages running diagonally against the plate would be subjected to have their wheels torn off, and the most serious accidents would result whatever precautions might be taken.'

[D K Clark quoting *The Observer* February 21 1858]

In London Train pursued his quest with unflinching zeal; a story which has been told and retold – with varying degrees of accuracy – over succeeding years. One of the most complete accounts is Charles Lee's paper referred to at footnote 6. However additional information has come to light from sources which were not available to him over fifty years ago.

Despite the failure of the 1858 attempt, all was not stacked against Train; some sections of the Press were very positive. 'The general scheme of these railways, as carried out in practice hitherto, consists of double lines of rails along the centre lines of the roads where there is a large omnibus traffic. The rails are laid so that vehicles of all kinds may cross them easily, and their principal use is to accommodate large passenger cars capable of holding fifty or sixty people each. ... The smoothness of the tramway renders travelling in such vehicles a positive enjoyment; we all know what enjoyment there is in the present jolting and jarring in omnibuses, and it is only a wonder that drivers and conductors are not wholly dislocated and dismembered before they arrive at sixty years of age. Perhaps they are, for no one sees an aged man on either box or monkey board, so we conclude they are put out of the way when the jarring has shaken them to pieces. One thing is certain, that it is impossible to read a newspaper in an omnibus, and a smooth, gliding transit, such as an invalid could endure would be a luxury ... There certainly needs to be a fair trial of it in London; one mile of rail would do it, and if it was found to be unsuited to our streets, and not adaptable to our habits, it could be taken up again with very little disturbance of the traffic, and the iron would be worth as much as before it went down, so that the possible expense of the experiment ought not to be considered.'[72]

Train initially adopted a broad brush approach and applied to many of the central London local government administrative bodies, generally at that time known as 'Vestries', with their members as Vestrymen. He is known to have contacted Marylebone, Islington, Clerkenwell, Lambeth and Southwark, and possibly others. Detailed records of more than one of the applications were rapidly published in pamphlet form which have reports of the often exceedingly verbose proceedings, and are accompanied by the equally wordy press reports.[73] In particular information is given[74] relating to Train's activities in his dealings with the St Mary's Lambeth Vestry relative to what was to become his third London tramway, the Surrey Side Street Rail Company Ltd. Detail is given of Vestry meetings between 5 November 1860 and 17 January 1861, with approval eventually given on the latter date after much discussion, for a single line just over a mile in length between the south end of Westminster Bridge and Kennington Gate (where a toll bar stood until 18 November 1865). Train's first letter of intent and request for permission to Lambeth Vestry was dated 9 August, and reports of subsequent meetings record that his proposals were favourably received.[75]

The Vestry of St Margaret's Westminster signified its agreement during September for a short line along Victoria Street from Broad Sanctuary to Vauxhall Bridge Road. On the basis of this authority, Train placed a second order for rolling stock, again with the Railway Carriage Company of Birmingham.[76] Like the first order, this was not to be fulfilled.

Next to respond to Train's advances was the Vestry of Marylebone, whose take on the matter was complicated by simultaneous applications, considered at the meeting on 6 October by Mr William J Curtis, who was first heard of in Liverpool, for permission to lay down his patent system, and also from the London General Omnibus Company, whose plans were then still in process of formulation. Train proposed that his line would run from St John's Wood, by Baker Street, Portman Square etc to Oxford Street and return up Oxford Street from Regent Street and through Gloucester Place and the New Road (sic) back to St John's Wood;[77] these initial ideas were then referred to a committee. Within a week this committee had heard that Curtis was prepared to lay down a demonstration line at his own cost, while Train was content to delay until the (undoubted) success of his Victoria Street line would put the matter beyond any doubt. The Vestry then agreed to proceed with the Train proposal.[78] However he quickly reduced his proposals to a line just the length of Oxford Street from Marble Arch to Tottenham Court Road, and even this was to be delayed until the Victoria Street line was proved successful.[79] Simultaneously Train's proposals were also under consideration by the Hackney Board of Works, who referred back the lines which were proposed to be laid in Newington Green, Southgate Road, Stam-

ford Hill, High Street Stoke Newington, Stoke Newington Road, High Street Dalston and Kingsland Road.[80] The Vestries of Paddington, Whitechapel and Camberwell delayed Train's advances without too much detailed consideration, also determining to wait to benefit from experience gained with the Victoria Street trial.[81] Hackney and Shoreditch did, however, agree to allow construction of a line from Ball's Pond Road by Dorchester Street to City Road at Ropemaker Street.

A list was published of eight lines proposed by Train; these were:

Regent Circus to Piccadilly and Kew; Oxford Street to Notting Hill; Bayswater by Marylebone, Euston and City to Moorgate Street; Bricklayer's Arms to Greenwich; Westminster Bridge to Clapham; Whitechapel to Stratford-le-Bow; London to Blackwall and Westminster Bridge to London Bridge by the new Southwark Road.[82]

At the end of October it was the turn of the City of London Commissioners to deal with Train's comprehensive proposals for tramways on many of the main thoroughfares within their jurisdiction. Streets to be utilised included Moorgate, Poultry, Cheapside, Cannon Street and Blackfriars Bridge. The matter was referred to committee.[83] A remarkable suggestion was that one of the longitudinal sleepers under the tram rail should be formed as a gas-pipe, thus avoiding the necessity to have separate excavations for both purposes. Nothing has been uncovered to suggest that this strange proposal was ever carried out.[84] On 30 October Train attended a court of the City [of London] Commissioners of Sewers and showed them a model of his proposed omnibus (seating 24 in and 24 out with a width of 6 ft 8 ins) and drawings of the street railway to a gauge of 4 ft 8½ ins. The Vestry of St George's Hanover Square was next to consider a list from Train of all the main thoroughfares within their sphere of interest which he considered were potential tram routes.[85] A special meeting was held, but again, with the imminent construction of the Victoria Street line, delay was instructed. This was also the decision of the Sewers' Commissioners when a letter from Train was debated on 11 December. He requested permission to extend into the City the line which he now had permission to construct from Hackney and Shoreditch Vestries. A six months pause was decided, again to learn from the experience of the other imminent lines.[86] His detailed proposal was for a connecting line from Ropemaker Street to the south end of Moorgate Street, where it there joined the line through Shoreditch and Hackney to Islington. Moorgate Street was to be single track with a passing place and Finsbury Place was proposed as double track.[87]

Train's frustration at the necessity to deal simultaneously with myriad public bodies, no two of which seemed inclined to either co-operate or even behave in an even handed manner, must have caused him considerable stress. However he was able to write to the Whitechapel Board of Works on 11 February 1861 confirming that physical work on the Marble Arch line would start in one week, that twenty carriages were nearing completion, and that he would be starting soon on four further lines for which he had permission, Pimlico to Westminster Abbey, Southgate Road Hackney, Moorgate Street City and Westminster Bridge to Kennington.[88]

Several references were included in Train's work (reference 45), including one worth quoting at length for the depth of detail included, which appears nowhere else;

'On Tuesday last, the ship 'Wyoming' which left this port for Liverpool, took with her the first of three Philadelphia-built street railroad cars for the new line about to be opened in London. The order for these cars was given by Mr Charles Hathaway, Esq., who has been in London for the last few weeks arranging for the general introduction of our railroad system there. So little time was given, that Messrs. Kimball and Gorton, to whom the order was sent, were compelled to send cars already

commenced for the Pittsburg city railroads. The Londoners, therefore, will have no more than a fair sample of our work, neither better nor worse than that which is exemplified wherever Philadelphia-built cars are running in this country. In describing the new car – the Prince Royal, as it is named – we are describing merely the type of the cars used in Cincinnati, Pittsburg, Baltimore, and Boston. The Prince Royal is smaller, and is built for a narrower guage [sic] than the Philadelphia cars, but it is as superior, in capacity, elegance, and comfort, to any public conveyance now running in London, as it is superior to a furniture waggon, to which a London omnibus may with propriety be compared. The Philadelphia street railroad guage is 5 ft. 2½ in., or 6 inches more than the 'narrow guage' of railroads generally, to which – the 4 ft. 8½ in. guage – the new London line corresponds. Our cars are reckoned as 22 passenger cars, (often carrying 50), while that under notice is rated as an 18 passenger car. The body is 14 ft. long, exclusive of the platforms, 7 ft. wide, and the height from the floor to the underside of the turtle-back roof is 7 ft. 6 in. The framing is of ash, which is lighter, stiffer, and less subject to shrinkage and warping than oak. The panelling is of white wood. The wheels are Whitney's 30 inches in diameter. The axles are from Pencoyd Works of A. & P. Roberts, of this city. The springs are of India rubber, which seems to answer the best purpose under the rough usage of street cars. The boxes are oil tight, a close packing being employed around the axle between the journal and the wheel. The brasses have a recess, on top, in which a hemispherical projection, on the inside of the upper part of the box, rests, forming a sort of ball and socket bearing. The pedestals (axle guards, the English mechanics will call them) are of cast-iron, and of the common pattern. The car has brakes, as usual. Inside, the finish is exceedingly plain, but neat. Like all American cars and omnibuses, and therefore unlike all conveyances of that kind in Edgland [sic], the windows extend all around the car. Each is a single large plate of American glass. Above each window is a gothic-shaped plate of ground glass, ornamentally figured, and relieving the entablature. The body is painted in lemon chrome, with arabesque ornaments on the sides, and the name, Prince Royal, in shaded skeleton letters below. The style of the whole is, of course, unlike anything in England, yet it is of that character which, familiarized as we are with it here, would be pronounced simple and appropriate. John Bull *may* pronounce it gaudy. The weight of the car is 3,462 lb., and it will comfortably afford sitting room for a dozen John Brights or two dozen little Lord John Russells. It is expected to be on the track by Christmas, when we have no doubt there will be a general turn-out among the parliamentary dignitaries of Westminster to see it. Our English readers will obtain an accurate idea of the appearance of the new car by referring to the cut in Messrs. Kimball and Gorton's card, in our advertising columns.'[89]

The *Wyoming*, it has been confirmed[90] did arrive in Liverpool, from Philadelphia, on 24 December 1860, but the name quoted for the tram element of the cargo seems an odd mixture of two names which were actually carried. '*Prince Royal*' is not a recognised title within the British monarchic system – but both '*Prince Consort*' and '*Princess Royal*' are. While apparently surprisingly detailed regarding other aspects of this shipment, how was it possible to misinterpret these titles?

The three cars would appear to be those supplied for Train's Marble Arch Street Railway, which is substantiated – in most respects – by the observations of the correspondent of an Irish newspaper 'The first London street railway opened last Saturday at 10 o'clock in a very quiet way … Marble Arch in the direction of Notting-hill, little more than a mile in

length. There is a single set of rails with a set of sidings at each end, and at intervals short curves strike off from the line and reunite with it again. The carriages are built by Messrs Prentiss & Co of Birkenhead – long and low with no seats on top. On Saturday three carriages were placed on the line, 'The Prince Consort' and 'The Princess Royal' first, and in about an hour afterwards 'Her Majesty' …'[91] It is not impossible that Prentiss arranged the import, and also the forwarding of the cars to London. Elijah Prentiss was an American chemist who joined Train in Birkenhead and had been persuaded to invest in that enterprise.[92]

No sooner had physical work commenced on the Marble Arch line than a vexatious summons was taken out at Marylebone Police Court by Alexander James Beresford Beresford Hope, 'that he [Train] did … unlawfully break up and injure the surface of a certain road … Uxbridge Road … being a turnpike-road contrary to the statute'. A labourer, Thomas Hutt, who was at work at the place, was also summoned. Hope gave evidence, stating that the rails would be highly dangerous to carriages and horses passing over, and that the height of the flange from the bed of the tramway plate was from one and a half to two inches, and that he thus considered it a nuisance. He thought it undesirable that these rails should be laid down on any turnpike road.[93] Some weeks later the Magistrate, Mr Yardley imposed a fine of 1/- on Train, but noted that either party could take the matter to a higher court and that he was not making a decision as to the principle behind the action; Train had been liable for breaking the road, and had never denied it, but had done it under licence of the appropriate authorities who had, in the magistrate's opinion, exceeded their powers. The tramway, he opined, caused no more inconvenience than passing over a loose stone.[94] Notice of appeal was lodged, but so far, no trace of this has been found.

Meantime the street railway had arrived in town; the Marble Arch line opened, after a construction period of just four weeks, on 23 March 1861. At 10 am the three cars started operation running along Bayswater Road from Marble Arch as far as Porchester Terrace. The almost exactly one-mile long line was of single

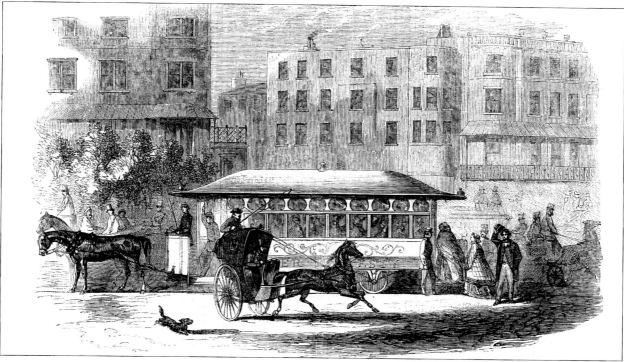

Top. The first London line was along Bayswater Road from Marble Arch. The crowds on the opening day *may* be exaggerated, but the line did excite great interest – and opposition from the carriage 'class', omnibus proprietors, and cab owners. From *'Illustrated London News'*.

Above. Possibly at the western terminus of the Bayswater line at Notting Hill the car *'Her Majesty'* is seen in a slightly more decorous situation. From *'Cassell's Illustrated Family Paper'*.

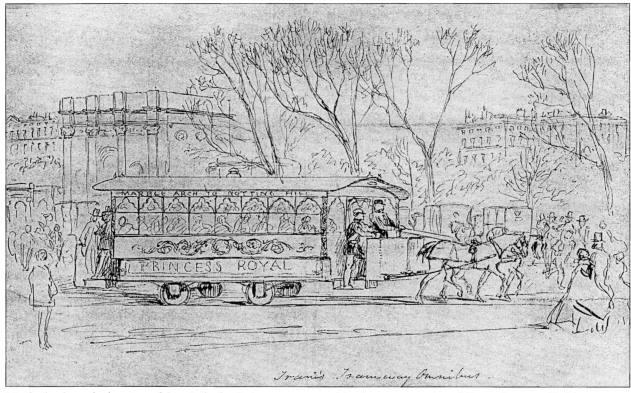

No doubt about the location of this nicely detailed contemporary sketch of the car *'Princess Royal'*. With the Marble Arch prominent behind the car, it is heading west with what appears to be a full complement of inside passengers plus a fair number on the rear platform. From *'Locomotion in Victorian London, Sekor, 1938'*.

track, on the south side of the road (where, with Hyde Park behind, there were no street crossings) with four sixty feet long sidings, one at each end and two intermediate. The cars were said to have been built by Prentiss of Birkenhead, and while they probably carried his name and may have been imported by him for Train, they were, in fact provided by Kimball & Gorton of Philadelphia – a fact which Train may have been anxious to disguise. At 2pm Train entertained some 350 gentlemen to a 'turtle luncheon' in St James's Hall, with many speeches and many toasts – although Train himself was an abstainer.[95] Thousands of spectators thronged the streets to watch or attempt to travel on this newest sensation. Numbers of labourers were deployed with brooms to sweep from the rails stones which 'mysteriously' seemed to manifest in a (sometimes successful) attempt to derail the vehicles. Cabs and other vehicles mounted a sustained campaign of interference. A fare of 2d was charged, but a challenge was soon mounted by the patent Curtis omnibus being brought to run on the same lines.[96]

Curtis's omnibus, *Enterprise*, had already been brought to London from Liverpool, and it would appear that he had every intention of promptly operating it on the newly laid tram line in Bayswater Road. However, at the beginning of April, the Inspector of Metropolitan Stage Carriages, declined to licence it 'until it had a table of fares and cushions for the roof seats'. Train's vehicles – it was said – were not licensed as they run under the Railway Act, and not as Metropolitan Hackney Carriages.[97] The vehicle remained in London, and was described – 'it asserts in large gold letters that it is fitted for 'the rail, the tramway, and the road'' and specified also that it ran from Marble Arch

Curtis's *'Enterprise'* omnibus (which had patent wheels to create the ability to operate on Train's rails) was used in Liverpool, then very briefly on two of Train's London lines. (From Patent 1071 of 1856)

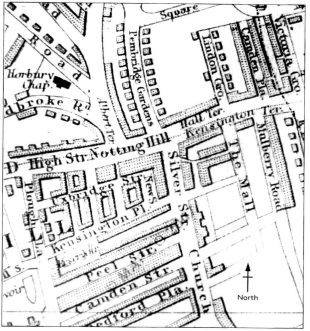

Detail from an early London street plan showing the location of Silver Street, where the Bayswater line cars were stabled.

to Notting-hill for one penny, thus undercutting the tramway.[98]

A short extension was laid into the yard of Richard Burden, coachsmith, in Silver Street (the north end of Church Lane, now Kensington Church Street) with the three vehicles kept in his shed.[99] Train had a

pamphlet amounting to over one hundred pages printed after the opening. An excoriating review of this read '... As an illustration of how far the bad taste, personal interest, and vain-glorification of one man can go, and as a painful example of how many among us are ready to endorse such vulgar egotism, the pamphlet is both instructive and curious.'[100]

Charles Hathaway, the Philadelphia engineer used by Train for construction of all of his lines, now commenced on the Victoria Street line, breaking the ground on 5 April. It had been intended that the track would commence at the new Victoria Station, but refusal by the Vestry of St George Hanover Square to allow the rails to cross a strip of the road under their jurisdiction meant that the terminus was some yards short of that point. Just under ¾ mile in length, the eastern terminus was in Broad Sanctuary by Westminster Abbey. The single track was laid to the north of the centreline of the street, with sidings at each end.[101] Again work progressed rapidly, with the line opened at 8 am on Monday 15 April, the occasion celebrated in the Westminster Palace Hotel, opposite the eastern terminus by an American breakfast. After the repast Mr Train announced his wish to have the company photographed in front of the hotel with the carriage in the foreground. 'The photographic operation completed, the company having retired from the windows returned to their seats ...'[102] This is the oft repeated scene with *'The People'* car, reproduced here yet again in two versions.

All three London tramways opened during 1861; the Marble Arch line on 23 March, the Victoria Street line on 15 April, and the Surrey Side line on 15 August (a fourth, along Southgate Road Hackney, was sanctioned, but construction never started). None of the 'temporary' concessions was extended beyond the initial period, and all traces were removed by the middle of the following year. This lack of success was probably exacerbated by Train's ability to rub people up the wrong way, plus his use of his (patented) step rail – although he, and others, contended that the grooved rail presented greater hazard. His own rail was refined quite rapidly, with the step reduced in height; had he used the

Train arranged for this photographic record to be made of the opening of his Victoria Street line. It was taken on 15 April 1861 near the Westminster terminus, with behind, the Westminster Palace Hotel and his guests to the 'Yankee Breakfast' at the windows. It is thought that the bearded figure on the platform (upper view) is Charles Hathaway, the American engineer who acted as contractor for all six of Train's lines in England. The lower photograph is less well known than the upper; in it Train is central in the window second from the right. (© London Transpost Museum)

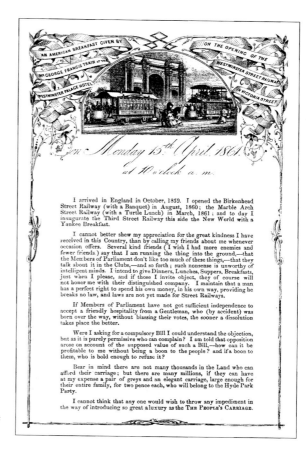

I arrived in England in October, 1859. I opened the Birkenhead Street Railway (with a Banquet) in August, 1860; the Marble Arch Street Railway (with a Turtle Lunch) in March, 1861; and to day I inaugurate the Third Street Railway this side the New World with a Yankee Breakfast.

I cannot better shew my appreciation for the great kindness I have received in this Country, than by calling my friends about me whenever occasion offers. Several kind friends (I wish I had more enemies and fewer friends,) say that I am running the thing into the ground,—that the Members of Parliament don't like too much of these things,—that they talk about it in the Clubs,—and so forth; such nonsense is unworthy of intelligent minds. I intend to give Dinners, Lunches, Suppers, Breakfasts, just when I please, and if those I invite object, they of course will not honor me with their distinguished company. I maintain that a man has a perfect right to spend his own money, in his own way, providing he breaks no law, and laws are not yet made for Street Railways.

If Members of Parliament have not got sufficient independence to accept a friendly hospitality from a Gentleman, who (by accident) was born over the way, without biassing their votes, the sooner a dissolution takes place the better.

Were I asking for a compulsory Bill I could understand the objection, but as it is purely permissive who can complain? I am told that opposition arose on account of the supposed value of such a Bill,—how can it be profitable to me without being a boon to the people? and if a boon to them, who is bold enough to refuse it?

Bear in mind there are not many thousands in the Land who can afford their carriage; but there are many millions, if they can have at my expense a pair of greys and an elegant carriage, large enough for their entire family, for two pence each, who will belong to the Hyde Park Party.

I cannot think that any one would wish to throw any impediment in the way of introducing so great a luxury as the THE PEOPLE'S CARRIAGE.

The front and inside pages of the menu for those lucky enough to be invited to the meal at the hotel. Its extent is quite remarkable, and no doubt the repast was not to be forgotten easily by the attendees. Note that the engraving has changed, with Bayswater and Paddington now become Westminster and Victoria , more relevant to the line being celebrated. (© National Tramway Museum)

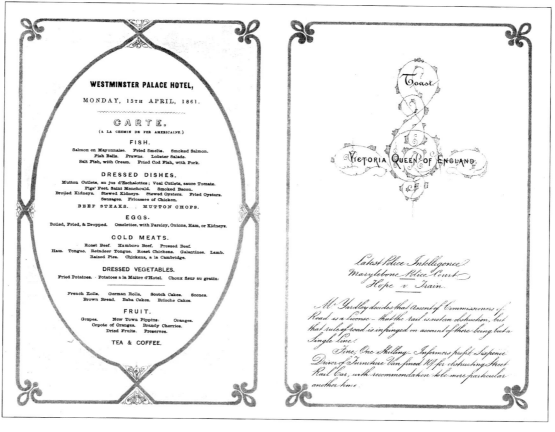

Left. Press report of the Victoria Street line opening which refers to the second car.

Below. Detail of the double-deck car *'Napoleon III'* which was produced for Train's promotional material. The double deck car which ran on Victoria Street may have resembled this sketch. It was constructed by the Railway Carriage Company of Oldbury, Birmingham, but was described as having spiral stairs to access the upper deck. Access to the upper deck initially formed a challenge which produced different solutions. Only after John Stephenson of New York patented his (widely copied) half turn stair was the upper deck accessible by ladies.

grooved rail and adapted it as conditions demanded the outcome may have been totally different.

Despite opposition – almost an automatic reaction from the 'carriage trade' – there were numerous users who found the new form of transport to be a distinct improvement over the old. Towards the end of May a

petition of several thousand signatures was presented to the Commissioners of Metropolitan Roads, in favour of a continuation of the Bayswater Road line to Shepherd's Bush, using double track. A survey was undertaken by Mr Prowse, chief surveyor of roads north of the Thames, of traffic on the lines under his jurisdiction. 'The number of passengers carried by one car on weekdays, and two on Sundays, on the Victoria-street line, since its opening on 15 April amounted to 31,500. On the Marble-arch line the two cars running on week days, and the three, and occasionally four, on Sundays, have yielded a return of £120 per week, which at 2d per head makes the number of passengers amount weekly to 14,400. The traffic on the latter line has so much increased during the past week that an extra carriage has been put on for permanent running.'[103]

Not everybody was – at least initially – completely antipathetic to Train's street railways.

'Among improvements recently suggested, is that of street railways. They have been tried and adopted in New York. Mr Train, an enterprising American, has introduced them to England, and the experiment is now being made between the Marble Arch and Notting-hill ... The carriages employed on the line are built on an American model, and bear no likeness to the vehicles to which we are accustomed in London. They have the appearance of being low-roofed and disproportionately long; they have no seats on the roof or driver's box; a platform, raised two feet from the ground, and guarded by a fence, is connected with the carriage at both ends. These are devoted to the use of the coachman and conductor, and perhaps two or three passengers. Each end of the carriage is fitted up so as to allow of the pole being inserted, and the horses harnessed without turning it round. The inside of the conveyance is comfortably arranged – a sufficiency of space being allotted to each passenger ... a bell communication between the driver and conductor, who, by the way, are clothed in a neat grey uniform. It was not without considerable difficulty that the experiment was tolerated, and the projector found himself persistently opposed by prejudice; but the plan was ultimately allowed to be tried, and

the lines were laid down accordingly. The inauguration ... was met, as may naturally be supposed, with a good deal of annoyance from rival 'busses and indignant cabs. The conservatism of those who were interested, commercially, in street conveyances, was shown by the determined hostility which they assumed to the American system. So far, however, as the experiment has been made, we understand the street railway has achieved a decided success ... That 'bus proprietors should be averse to rivalry ... is not at all unlikely; but the question is differently regarded by the riding public – they require better treatment than they have yet received, and they will have it. If Mr Train's street railway is found really successful, the system will be generally adopted, and the omnibus proprietors must emulate their American competitor, not by impeding his progress, but by starting a train of their own. Whether they will ever successfully compete with their shrewd and enterprising rival is a thing of which, judging from their present style of management, we are far from hopeful'.[104]

Another paean came from an unlikely source

'... the boon is a great one, and we hail the day now so rapidly approaching, when England will share in the many benefits of the street railway; but we are not in the least surprised to find that, like all other labour-saving inventions, it has first to run the gauntlet of prejudice, ignorance and that stupid form of conservatism that looks upon every change as an innovation. Thus we know that certain towns in England petitioned Parliament that no railroad should be made within a certain distance from their boundary lines, and now they have to pay the penalty in the stagnation of their trade ...'[105]

Most of the cars supplied for the three London

Above. Imposing architecture of Westminster with a diminutive representation of *'The People'* tram heading for the terminus in Broad Sanctuary.

Right. Enlarged detail from the above scene.

tramways appear to have come from America. Prentiss of Birkenhead is more than once given the credit in contemporary accounts for those built for the Marble Arch line, and these may have carried his plate (perhaps as 'supplier').[106] Even Train said they were by Prentiss, but he was probably trying to minimise the US input. However the detailed description above appears to show unequivocally that they were fabricated in Philadelphia. The single deck car '*The People*' for the Victoria Street line was probably also constructed in Philadelphia. However Train had already (prematurely) placed an order for four large top-seat cars for his planned Birmingham line from R W Johnson's Railway Carriage Company Ltd of Oldbury by Birmingham.[107] The completed vehicle was referred to in the contemporary technical press.[108] One car was complete by the beginning of October, and it was reported to have been taken on a 'trial trip' to Westminster on Saturday 6 October 1860 for exhibition to the public – this some months before track laying commenced![109] It was then described as 'a huge omnibus to run on the iron tramway from Broad Sanctuary to Vauxhall Bridge Road …carries 58 passengers in and out, the outside seats being approached by a spiral staircase.[110] It is, however, not impossible that this was a journalistic misinterpretation as – despite generally giving Train a favourable press at this time – it would appear that none of the London based daily newspapers covered the event.

Two press reports give considerable insight;[111] [112]

The expansion of the street railway system in this country has called into requisition a new style of carriage, which promises to supersede on all well-frequented roads, the cribbed, cumbersome, and confined old-fashioned omnibus. Some vehicles of this description intended for the London street railway, laid down from the Marble Arch to Kensington, by Mr G F Train, have recently been manufactured at the Railway Carriage Company's works, at Oldbury, near Birmingham. A few months since several street railway omnibuses were built at this establishment for the proposed street railway in this town extending from Monument Lane, Edgbaston to the end of New Street; but as the adoption of Mr Train's system in Birmingham has been deferred to a more convenient season, the carriages have not yet been required, and probably the citizens of Bristol or some other provincial capital will be shortly privileged to enjoy the vehicular comforts which our townsmen have failed to secure. The street railway omnibuses have, however, undergone a material change for the better since the first vehicles of the kind were constructed. We recently had an opportunity of inspecting one of these, comprising all the modern improvements, at the company's works at Oldbury. It is of capacious dimensions, being about 6 ft 6 ins in height, the same in width, and about 16 ft in length. The exterior of the omnibus is painted blue, with a gold scroll combining the well-known emblems of the rose, shamrock, and thistle, designed by Mr Owen Jones. The interior exhibits a spacious saloon, at once lofty, commodious and well ventilated. Here, notwithstanding the amplitude of female attire sanctioned by the conventionalities of modern fashion, eighteen persons can be seated as inside passengers, there being plenty of room for persons to walk upright from end to end, without touching or incommoding those who sit on either side of the omnibus. The fittings are of an elegant description, much superior to some of the first-class saloons on railways, and there is an apparatus, easy of access, by means of which each passenger can readily ring a bell calling the conductor. The top, or 'knife-board,' has outside accommodation for twenty-two passengers. A very simple break, affixed at each end of the carriage, enables either the driver or conductor to bring the vehicle to a standstill in less time than the horses attached to an ordinary omnibus can be pulled up.

On Monday we had an opportunity of seeing the new carriages in process of building at Mr Johnson's railway carriage works, Oldbury, destined for Mr Train's street lines in London and Birkenhead. Saving that they are light, elegant, and commodious vehicles, and somewhat larger than an ordinary omnibus, there is nothing strikingly novel in their construction. The carriages we saw, one of them in a completed state, measured about twenty-two feet in length, and a little more than eight feet wide, the exact length of space within being eighteen feet. There is accommodation in the interior for eighteen persons, or one foot per individual, not an extravagant space when the prevailing fashion in attire is taken into account, and on the outside are seats for a similar number. ... ample space between the cushioned seats ... Access to the top is gained by spiral steps. The only desideratum we would wish to see within the carriages is the partitioning off of the seats, as this would avoid the overcrowding inseparable from common benches, no matter what number they are 'licensed to carry.' Some provision should also be made to shelter the outsiders from bad weather, as on the chemin de fer Americain in the suburbs of Paris. As regards the make of the vehicles, they are far superior to anything of the kind yet produced, and Mr Train, we understand, has on his line some specimens of American 'vans' which will ill bear comparison with these of Oldbury. Some notion of the completeness with which Mr Johnson's carriages are built may be gathered from the fact that the largest sized ones – those whose dimensions we have specified – will cost Mr Train something over £200, or about double the cost of a common street omnibus, and two-thirds the cost of an ordinary first-class railway carriage. One or two of the carriages at the Oldbury works are richly decorated, on the designs of Mr Owen Jones – perhaps over

decorated, considering the use to which they are to be applied; but this is an error which concerns the purchaser alone. The carriages are all four-wheelers – the wheels being quite as small as those on our railway trucks – and will be drawn by two horses, one horse pulling on rails doing usually about five times as much work as one horse pulling on the road. In the matters of light and ventilation, every provision is made for the convenience of the 'insides.'

It would appear convincing that the most complete of the Oldbury built vehicles referred to was actually that which was taken to London and used on the Westminster line. This may be confirmed by an action raised by Richard Johnson, proprietor and managing director of the Railway Carriage Company, in September 1861, petitioning to wind up the Westminster Street Railway Company who, he claimed, had not paid him the £250 cost of the omnibus made and *delivered*. The matter was held over until January 1862. No further record has been found, the matter probably being resolved out of court.[113] There are other references to this double-deck car on the Victoria Street line, but no specific details of it have been found.[114] However in late November 1861, an accident was reported, involving 'the large car' of the Westminster Company.[115] On the Surrey Side line three, and on occasions, four cars were in use. It is of course not impossible that 'spare' cars were moved between the lines as traffic demands required.

A press reference later stated that Train was making about £10 per day from each car on the Bayswater line, almost three times the earnings anticipated from any omnibus. Also 'He has 40 great cars coming from America, built on the true New York principle, which Mr Train has found it impossible to make our coachbuilders understand; and the cost of importing will be a saving of 25% on manufacturing'.[116] It would appear that Train was already less than satisfied with the cars built by Main in Birkenhead. While the '40 cars' may be a typical exaggeration, the sentiment is probably an accurate reflection, as only the six earliest cars (four for Birkenhead and two for Sydney) can be definitely attributed to Robert Main. For his next batch of cars Train appears to have reverted to the tried and tested American suppliers. At the end of November 1860, a report stated 'A firm in Philadelphia have just finished a railroad car for the Birkenhead Street Railway opposite Liverpool. It is similar to those built for the roads in Philadelphia. The weight of the car is 3575 pounds, and its cost about $900. The builders of the car intend to put in estimates for the construction of all the cars to be run on the English passenger road.'[117]

Train frequently made the assertion that his line of rails was not for his sole benefit, and this was put to the test when an opposing vehicle was indeed put on the track. This was the Curtis omnibus from Liverpool which had an adjustable flange on the leading wheels to enable it to benefit from the tracks, and to also run with the flange removed, on the road formation. The wheel 'gauge' of most horse buses then in use was about twelve inches wider than Train's rails. William Curtis was a prolific inventor, and his patent for the 'improved omnibus' had been registered in May 1856. Operation of one Curtis patent omnibus commenced in Liverpool on the 'Line of Docks' railway during March 1859, with some degree of success, but ended early in the following year.[118] One of these – double deck with 45 seats – was taken to London in early September 1860, said to for the United Kingdom Tramway Company who had approval for an initial line in Islington.[119] However in April 1861 the vehicle made unprecedented use of the rails of the Marble Arch Street Railway; 'A few days ago a monster omnibus with portable flanges on the two leading wheels, the invention of Mr Curtis, titled the *Enterprise,* drawn by four grey horses, made its unexpected appearance upon the tramway, and plied for passengers in opposition to the cars of Mr Train, at the same fare – viz., 2d. per head. Although this novel omnibus was capable of accommodating a larger number of passengers than the cars, was decorated with the Union Jack, signifying it to be an English invention, and therefore not an American like its opponent, and alleged to possess a great advantage, by being so constructed as to run with equal facility on and off the tram, it was

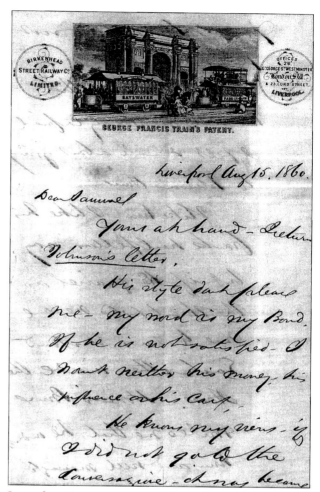

Letter from Train to the engineer James Samuel indicating use of the Marble Arch engraving as a letterhead.

certainly nothing like as well patronised as each of the cars, which were crammed with passengers every journey ...'[120] Curtis's *Enterprise* was also used on the Surrey Side line, operating from the top of Kennington Road to Westminster at half the tram fare, and was involved there in a fatal accident which may have resulted in its withdrawal.[121]

Sir Benjamin Hall [later the first Lord Llanover] who is frequently cast as senior condemnator of all London tramway proposals, was Chief Commissioner of Public Works at the hearing into the 1857 Bill introduced by the London Omnibus Tramway Company,

Sir John Villiers Shelley, Bart MP – pillar of the establishment.

Sir Benjamin Hall MP – implacable opponent of tramways.

and to him is ascribed the credit for the Bill's rejection. The oft-quoted reason for this resulted from damage caused to his carriage wheels when crossing a colliery tramway in his Welsh constituency. He was totally unable to accept that Train's proposals would be any improvement on that eighteenth century style hazard.

Charles Lee in his paper refers to a letter from Joseph Nelson which[122] states 'The indiscreet charge brought by Mr Train against Sir John Shelley was fatal to our progress in London …' [The charge was not, in fact, brought by Train, but by Richard Stafford, his landlord – but with Train and his family prominent participants throughout.] Opposition to Train and tramways in general is always referred to in regard to the indefatigable antagonism of Sir Benjamin Hall, but in Sir John Shelley, Train made another equally intransigent and exceedingly influential enemy. It is difficult

from this distance in time to follow Train's reasoning in pursuing the course he took, but it undoubtedly reinforced all the prejudices held against him as a 'pushy' American. This action almost certainly ensured the subsequent refusal by all Vestries involved to permit any extension of the periods agreed for operations.

Train's lodgings were then at 18 St James's Street, almost opposite the apartments of Sir John Villiers Shelley, Bart, MP at number 66. In the middle of June 1861 Sir John was charged, probably at Train's instance, at Marlborough Street Police Court with indecent conduct. It was stated that he had exposed 'his person' at the first floor window on more than one occasion, and in full view of Train's wife, servants and other ladies, and if the behaviour was not suppressed it would render the property impossible to let. The event was stated to have taken place when the ladies were gath–

ered at the upstairs window to view the carriages passing to the Queen's drawing-room and on subsequent occasions. On 19 June Train wrote to Sir John 'Sir – I have the misfortune to occupy apartments opposite yours. You have a perfect right, as a public man, to oppose in parliament or in the commissioners' boards my street railway; but you have no right, as a private individual, to insult my wife, my guests, my landlady, or my servants, by such a disgraceful exhibition as you have been guilty of this morning during the Queen's drawing-room. Unless you send me an instant and ample apology for your most ungentlemanly conduct, I will not only hold you personally responsible, but give you a publicity you never contemplated". Sir John's immediate written reply was insufficient to placate the outraged parties. 'Sir – I am in receipt of your letter of this day, and shall be obliged to you to inform me to what you refer beyond the fact of my having, on public grounds, objected to the establishment of tramways in the streets of the metropolis. If inadvertently I have done anything which can by possibility have caused any annoyance to any one, in consequence of my windows having been open during the extreme heat of the day – especially if any lady has been annoyed – you will find me anxious to make every apology. My apology will be that I was not aware that I could be overlooked, and that I shall take care that, however stifling, my windows be closed in future.''[123] [124] The matter was then taken to the Police Court.

The more salacious details are not relevant to this study, but were nevertheless given in considerable detail for the enlightenment of prurient Victorians.[125] Not only was Sir John a respected Member of Parliament, representing the Westminster constituency, he was a magistrate, and a colonel in the Middlesex Volunteers. The magistrate hearing the case, Mr Corrie, dismissed the charge, declaring that Sir John left with his character unblemished; as it was inconceivable that a gentleman and a magistrate would behave in the manner alleged, and that he did not believe the evidence of the witnesses, '... it was all an illusion'.[126] 'Sir John ... as he went to a conveyance waiting for him, was received with huzzas from many hundred persons waiting the

event outside the Court, whilst the witnesses for the defence left the spot in cabs, assailed by the most tremendous yells and hisses.'[127] A more temperate report ended '...of Mr Train, we simply think that he showed want of delicacy and discretion in being quick to believe and support a story that, even before disproof, was utterly incredible.'[128]

While this was being dragged through the courts, construction of Train's third London line was progressing, although delayed by a strike of ironworkers at Ebbw Vale where the rails were made. The General Surveyor of the Metropolitan Roads Board, Mr H Browse, reported in a completely favourable mien on the Bayswater tramway. His comments – the considered opinion of a professional – rather than the biased opinion of one with a vested interest, make interesting reading. He reported; 'I do not consider there is any danger in this tramway; the inconvenience to general traffic is very trifling; from the novelty of the invention some annoyance has no doubt been caused to the inhabitants along the line, but that novelty is fast abating and will soon cease; it appears that some 12,454 persons availed themselves of this means of conveyance (on that line, two cars running) in the week ending the 5th June, being the sixth week from the first opening of the tramway; and I feel convinced that if a double line were laid down, and extended to Palace Gardens-road, that number would be greatly increased, the number of omnibuses would be diminished, and consequently a saving would accrue in the cost of repairing and maintaining the road'.[129] Unfortunately these positive words failed to influence the relevant authority. A memorial was submitted on 20 June to the Commissioners of Turnpike roads north of the Thames by a large number of prominent local residents (including Sir John Shelley and Lord Portman) who claimed that the line had caused a number of accidents, and that 'it must be contrary to the wishes of the commissioners as it contrary to the public interest ... and that as an experiment it had been a mistake and a failure as regards the public'.[130] At a further meeting on 5 July, by a large majority, the Commissioners then decided that the Bayswater Road rails must be removed and the road restored to its original condition by 4 October.[131]

This announcement created considerable public discontent, and a public meeting on 9 August was called in an endeavour to have the decision reversed, which passed a resolution;

'That, in the opinion of this meeting the Bayswater Street Railway is a most convenient and agreeable method of travelling, and a great improvement on the previous mode of conveyance.

... from the construction of the carriages, their commodious and elegant arrangements, they furnish to the public an amount of accommodation and comfort unknown in any other public street conveyance.

... the fact of the carriages being under the complete control of the driver, enables all persons, even the aged and infirm, to enter and leave them without the least danger of accident.

... this meeting has heard with great regret and astonishment that the Commissioners of Metropolitan Roads have passed a resolution to deprive the public of this great improvement.

... a committee be appointed to wait upon the Commissioners, and to take such steps as they may think requisite to induce the honourable board to rescind their resolution and preserve the Bayswater Street railway to the public.

An amendment however proposed '... that this meeting is of the opinion that the Commissioners are deserving of the thanks of the public for ordering the removal of Mr Train's street railway from this populous thoroughfare'. A vote showed forty or fifty hands for this amendment, and many hundreds against it, with the motion then declared carried 'amidst loud and prolonged cheering and some marks of disapproval'.[132]

A meeting of the Vestry of St George's Hanover Square during July had earlier received an application by the Westminster Street Railway Co for permission to lay rails in Victoria Street, Vauxhall Bridge Road, Eaton Street, Grosvenor Place and Kensington Road; after considerable debate the request was refused.[133]

Train's third London line opened after the instruction had been given that the first was to be closed. On Thursday 15 August the Surrey Side Street Railway commenced operation with a car 'The Army' running from Kennington Park along Kennington Road and Westminster Bridge road as far as Mount Street. The last few yards were incomplete then, and the short length to the south end of Westminster Bridge opened soon after.[134] Unfortunately, after only a few weeks' use, a 14-year old boy was killed, having fallen (possibly pushed) from the front platform of another car, 'Hope'.

Contemporary Press advertisement for the Surrey Side Street Railway, indicating its potential for links to the Express Boats on the Thames for rapid access to the City.

No blame was attached by the coroner to the driver, and Train, who attended the investigation (and who was on the car when the accident happened) advised that in the three weeks running some 46,000 passengers had been carried, and that this was the only accident. He had arranged for wire guards to be fitted round the wheels. The coroner recommended that no passenger should travel on the front platform.[135]

By the time the Shelley affair had been dragged through the courts, Train's Marble Arch tram had only a few weeks' operation to run, instructions having been issued by the Metropolitan Roads Commissioners that it was to be removed by 4 October 1861. Work on lifting the timbers and rails started on 11 September, working in from the western terminus, with the cars remaining in operation for a further day or two until the remaining length was too short to justify this. The precise date of the final run – the first tramway abandonment in England – appears to have escaped the record. Even the local newspapers were undecided: on the same day was published '... several navvies were employed on removal of the iron rails. They began operations near Notting-hill and as the rails were taken up the gravel was relaid. Mr Train's carriages however continue to run upon the part of the line which remains ...'[136] – then – '... the cars have now discontinued running upon it, preparatory to its removal... '[137] As the first of these references is from a weekly paper, and the second from a daily, it seems reasonable to assume that the latter has a better chance of accuracy, and that operations ceased on or about the 19th and certainly by the 21st. It would not have taken a great deal of effort to lift the short and relatively lightly constructed line. On the 21st it was also announced 'Arrangements are concluded for Mr Charles Hathaway of Philadelphia, the street-railway contractor, to transfer the metals and timber of the tramway in Bayswater-road to the Surrey side of the water, to form part of a connecting link of street-railways from the Victoria and Pimlico Railway-stations to Blackfriars and London Bridges.'[138] This would appear to have been a forlorn hope.

At the end of October, the Hackney Board of Works, who had given permission to Train for a tramway along Southgate Road took cold feet in the light of events elsewhere and withdrew their permission before any physical work was undertaken.[139]

It seems however, that Train had already sealed his own fate with a letter to the Editor of the *New York Herald* in November 1861 which was promptly noted and reprinted in England. In it he intemperately accused every element of English [sic] society, from the army, the navy, the church, the administration, the banks and the aristocracy to unbridled support for, and overt collusion with, the secessionist aspirations of the southern states of America. To this the *Morning Chronicle* responded with a 1400 word leading article which set the tone for subsequent events.

'The instincts of a whole people are seldom wrong. For years past there has been growing in England an involuntary dislike of the being which calls itself a Yankee ... there is a man now lodging in St James's-street, who, uniting in his own person everything that is ridiculous in the general demeanour of a Yankee, is enjoying our hospitality and availing himself of our generosity to act the spy and insult us in the most ribald journals of New York. This individual is Mr GEORGE FRANCIS TRAIN, somewhat notorious with the tramway nuisance in our public thoroughfares. We shall not lay to his account the numerous fatal or otherwise lamentable accidents which have occurred since his pestilent enterprise was first taken into favour by certain vestries, nor is it necessary to hold him responsible for all the injuries inflicted by his abominable rails upon carriage springs; but by what right is it that he corresponds with that degraded purveyor of filth, the Editor of the *New York Herald*? Ever since he arrived in England, this TRAIN has been an offence, and, so to speak, a social obstruction. He has given champagne breakfasts to all who were incautious or abject enough to partake of them; he has exhibited himself in attitudes the vulgarity of which would have disgraced a booth at a rural fair; he has delivered speeches, the egotism of which was only less revolting than his notion that an English Member of Parliament could be bribed with a bucketful of iced wine; [etc, etc, etc] … But the matter assumes a very different complexion when we read his letter inserted in the vilest print of New York. He all but confesses that he is in communication with the spies who are sneaking about Southampton; he alludes to them as 'detectives''; he keeps an inventory of our ships cargoes … and we want to know if the English people are to endure his rowdy presence any longer.

… On no account let Mr TRAIN be put under the pump. We are very anxious not to have his windows broken. But we do say that no English gentleman can in future sit under the same roof with him, and we are glad to remember that there are journalists attached to the Press of this country who, from the first, refused every invitation to wallow at his bribery breakfasts … [etc, etc, etc] is this the sort of business that the tramway promoter has in England? We had thought that he confined his ambition to spoiling our streets, running down our omnibuses, jolting our cabs, damaging our broughams, and occasionally varying the performance by fracturing the legs of an old beggar or a few children. So long as the English public thought this harmless, Mr Train might safely take advantage of our hospitality … [he] is of a type of the Yankees we have depicted him, and his letter is in precise accordance with all that is abrasive, vain-glorious, ill-bred and impudent [etc]. … We recommend the volunteer correspondent of the New York Herald to adopt a pseudonym in his future communications, or, still better, to occupy himself in taking up his trams, which are not wanted in England. … Mr GEORGE FRANCIS TRAIN, his photographs, his speeches, his breakfasts, his cards, his omnibuses, his slang, his petitions, his puffs, have long been standing nuisances; but we can put up with a nuisance. Putting up with a spy is another matter.'[140]

Feelings regarding the Civil War in America (which commenced by the battle of Fort Sumter in the middle of April 1861, following secession of the eleven Southern states to form the Confederate States of America) were running high, with, at this time, the possibility of the UK entering on the side of the south being seriously proposed. Train, from the north, made no bones about where his allegiances lay, and in his famously outspoken manner, took every opportunity to further the cause. England, with major trade links with the cotton-producing south, tended to favour the south.

Train had by this time turned his attention away from the capital and made several overtures elsewhere, including Darlington and the Potteries. Another proposal, supported by Mr F Eggar, a prominent local landowner, was for a 4-mile line linking Aldershot and Farnborough in Hampshire. This, it was intended, would have branch lines to serve the north and south army camp areas. Despite Train receiving a good reception, and formation of a committee to further the idea, nothing tangible resulted.

At a meeting of the Board of Works for the Westminster Vestry on 10 February 1862, a decision was arrived at to instruct Mr Train to remove the line from Victoria Street, as soon as possible. This followed a concerted campaign of complaint against the line – mostly by parties with a vested interest. The line was said to be a dangerous nuisance and an interference with other traffic.[141] Although not stated, one can feel the malevolent influence of Sir John Shelley and his friends at work lobbying their influential associates. The line had to be removed and the road reinstated by the middle of March; final operation was on 6 March.

George Starbuck, in his capacity as managing director of the Surrey Side Street Railway at this time issued some interesting statistics relating to operation of the line; from 15 August to March 15, Miles run,

47,760; Passengers carried, 596,799; average number of cars in use, 3¾; passengers per car daily, 663; daily average takings per car, £5.3s; total receipts, 34455.6s4d; tickets in circulation, 6963.[142] In doing this he was making public information which was intended to justify the continuing existence of the line (and of his own position).

Problems with Lambeth Vestry persisted relative to the remaining tram line, [Shelley at work again?] with a bond demanded from Train of £1000 to meet potential legal expenses in defending an action following the issue of a joint indictment against Train and the Vestry for 'conspiracy and for causing a public nuisance in the Kennington Road by laying down iron rails thereon and thereby impeding the passage of, and inconveniencing, the public'. The prosecution had been instigated by a Mr Gregg, clerk of the peace for the county of Surrey 'not in his official capacity but merely as one of the public with a view to put a stop to what he considered a dangerous public nuisance ...' Train responded that he thought he had done all possible to meet the demands of the Vestry, and when he had offered cash security the vestry had taken a bond; he had removed two sidings to which objection had been raised, and continued 'I was not aware that my opinions or my politics were on trial, but simply my tramway ... I was in hopes that the unhappy irritation between our respective lands would not estrange me from Englishmen whom I respect, simply because I am an American."[143] The matter was referred back to committee.

The case was heard before a jury at Kingston during the first week of April 1862, and despite it being led that a petition of over 11,000 names had been presented in favour of the tramway being allowed, Train was found guilty and fined £500. The Chief Justice opined 'If ninety nine persons went safe, but the hundredth was endangered or suffered inconvenience from an act of this description, that would, according to my view of the law, support the charge before the court.[144] No time was lost by the victors; at 4 am on 20 June 'a party of 20 men ... commenced tearing up the rails. On Wednesday [17th] the warrant was placed in the hands of the sheriff for execution, but at the solic-

Surrey-side Street Railway Company (Limited).
18, Great George-street, Westminster.

NOTICE is hereby given, that at an Extraordinary General Meeting of the above Company, held at the Registered Offices of the Company, 18, Great George-street, Westminster, on Thursday, the 24th day of October ultimo, voluntarily Resolutions were passed for the purpose of winding-up the affairs of the said Company, and appointing a Liquidator. And that at an adjourned Extraordinary General Meeting of the said Company, held at the Registered Offices aforesaid, on Monday, the 3rd day of November instant, Resolutions were passed confirming the said Resolutions of the aforesaid Extraordinary General Meeting of the 24th day of October ultimo.

The said Company is in consequence in process of being wound-up accordingly, and said Liquidator is duly appointed—Dated this 4th day of November, 1862.

J. G. Oliver, Secretary of the aforesaid Surrey-side Street Railway Company (Limited).

All claims on the above Company to be addressed to G. Starbuck, Jun., Old Broad-street, London; endorsed for Liquidator of the said Company.

Notice from 'the London Gazette' of 7 November 1862 relative to the winding up of the Surrey Side Company. No photographic illustration has been found of this line.

itation of Mr Train it was allowed to remain in abeyance until yesterday. The workmen began at the Triangle and went on working towards Kennington-park. Today a large additional number of workmen will be engaged, and will work up to Westminster-bridge. The cars were running yesterday for the last time from the Triangle to the bridge'.[145]

And so the last of Train's three London tramways came to an inglorious end. The antagonism of the carriage classes and the vociferous opposition of the omnibus proprietors ensured the inevitable conclusion. Large numbers of passengers had been carried, and, if nothing else, the superiority of metal wheels on metal rails had been proved over other forms of road traction. The horse bus was no competition for the horse tram. Within a decade, with but a minor adjustment to rail design, the principle returned to London's streets, with the first of a new generation of street tramways.

Even that esteemed journal *Punch* got in on the act, publishing 'The Vestry Fiat'

> To your new-fangled ways and means
> We still prefer our stale ways:
> We'll neither have street-railway trains,
> Nor yet have TRAIN'S street-railways.[146]

Train subsequently stated 'I built a street railway in Geneva, Switzerland ... and one in Copenhagen ... I also suggested the road in Bombay, India.' The 2 mile line from Place de Neuve in Geneva to Carouge was constructed and operated under a concession granted to a company registered by Charles Burn CE of London (author of *On the construction of Horse Railways for Branch Lines and for Street Traffic*). Where Train's connection came in is unclear (if it did exist). The initial six, seven-window saloon, cars supplied were very similar to the style of the Birkenhead double deck cars, and were constructed by Prentiss (described as the 'Street Rail Car Works at Birkenhead').[147] This line – with a fifty-year lease – opened on 19 June 1862.[148] It was laid from the start with a grooved rail of a design patented by Burn in 1860. Although in Bombay a concession was awarded for horse trams in 1866, the first line there did not open until 9 May 1874, with no known participation by Train.

Although Charles Burn has been mentioned by Train as his 'contractor", the London based civil engineer was ahead of Train in several respects. In 1859 he

A wintery St Petersburg view of early horse trams at Bolshoi Gostiny Dvor (the Great Guest Court, an immense grouping of shops founded in 1748), with the tower of the Duma behind, on Nevsky Prospekt. The tramway along the famous street was mostly single in horse car days, with groups of cars proceeding in convoy. The top deck looks exceedingly chilly! Although similar to contemporary cars built in England, it has not yet been possible to establish their manufacturer.

Above. Charles Burn's concession for the street railway from the centre of Geneva to Carouge initially used cars built in Birkenhead, possibly ordered through the General Rolling Stock Company. This scene, in la place de Neuve shows one of the original seven window saloon cars. The top deck seating is supported on to the sides of the car, as detailed in Prentiss's 1860 Patent.

Right. Press notification of the opening of Burn's Geneva tramway.

Below. Brass token used on the Carouge line.

Chemin de fer américain.
GENÈVE-CAROUGE

Le service de cette voie s'ouvrira pour le public le jeudi 19 courant, à midi. Les départs auront lieu provisoirement toutes les huit minutes, de la place du Marché à Carouge, et de la place Neuve à Genève.

Prix des places : 10 centimes.

Les omnibus prendront et déposeront les voyageurs tout le long du parcours de la ligne.

Les jetons, valables pour une course, se vendent dès aujoud'hui :

A Genéve, chez M. Huller, M⁴ de tabacs, à la Corraterie.

A Carouge, chez M. Lagrange, M⁴ de tabacs, place du Marché, et aux salles d'attente, au prix de 8 fr. le cent.

Un avis ultérieur donnera de plus amples indications sur l'horaire.

obtained a concession which had been granted two years earlier by the French Government to a M Boyer Bardy for a Loubat-style American horse-tramway in the Auvergne from Clermont-Ferrand to Riom, a distance of 15 kilometres (9¼ miles). To finance this he formed the 'Anglo-French Tram Railroad Co Ltd' which he claimed to be the first English tramway company registered in London. Unfortunately London financiers did not support his endeavour and the concession lapsed without any work being undertaken on the ground. However Burn claimed that this concession formed the model for subsequent continental tramways, including his successful line from Geneva to Carouge.[149]

The capital of Russia, St Petersburg (until 1918), saw a local Horse Railway company formed at the beginning of October 1862, which formally opened its first route on 8 September 1863. Two further routes opened later in that year, with a total length of 5 miles. The first delivery of cars (which were probably built in England) is said to have totalled 29, of the 'imperial' style, i.e. with top deck seats, carrying 22 inside and 24 on top. Because of the vertical stairs – and potential immodesty – women were not allowed to travel on the outside seats, until the stairs were altered and the ban removed on 17 March 1903.[150] A reference states that the first of the two St Petersburg horse tramway companies was established and financed 'almost entirely' by the Swiss consul to the city, eventually operating four lines.[151] The cars may have been built in England, as early in November 1864, a lighter from the steamship *Dwina* (ex London) carrying 'a street railway omnibus' was damaged by ice on the River Neva in St Petersburg. Despite carrying 1½ million passengers in the first year of operation (1864), the venture was not profitable and it passed to financiers Erlanger & Co of London and Paris in 1875. It has not been possible to link this to Train, and his singular reference to tramways in St Petersburg appears to have been made in his speech to the British Association in Oxford in July 1860, "That clumsy bungling affair [in Paris] gives no better idea of the real Horse Railway than does the *chemin de fer Americain* on the Neva's banks at St Petersburg ..."

He implies then that this was already in operation, but authoritative records quote the date above for the first tramway in the then Russian imperial capital.

Another undertaking with which it has been suggested Train claimed an association was the United Kingdom Railway Rolling Stock Company. This was floated in December 1862; some months after Train quit England, and was established to lease rolling stock to fledgling operating companies. The articles read 'It is not intended that the company shall be builders, or that any capital should be sunk in workshops or materials. The Rolling Stock will be purchased of the ordinary builders, as the circumstances of each contract may require ...'[152] J T Pritchell, a director of this company, was on the initial board at formation of the Copenhagen Railway Company on 1st June 1863 hence it is highly probable that the first six vehicles used there were leased from this undertaking, and were also built by Prentiss. This Rolling Stock Coy recorded its first business in mid 1863 and traded successfully for several years, regularly paying dividends of 6% or 7%. It was placed in liquidation in December 1871.[153]

What became of the vehicles used on the three London tramways has long intrigued transport historians; could it perhaps be that this company – the United Kingdom Railway Rolling Stock Company – was formed to deal with this matter? There is the potential (and totally logical suggestion) that some of the cars could have been re-cycled elsewhere, but an intriguing statement was recorded by the 'London Correspondent' of a west-country newspaper, reporting on the opening of the Great International Exhibition on 1st May 1862; 'At an early hour large numbers of carriages were slowly defiling towards [South Kensington] ... Vehicles of all descriptions – colossal omnibuses from Manchester; street tramway carriages dislodged from the iron pathway by indignant vestries; old seedy packing cases long since taken from the regular traffic ... now freshened up with a little paint and plastered with placards announcing that the Exhibition was their destination bore crowds of season-ticket holders ...'[154] The conversion of the street railway carriages for use as omnibuses has not previously been alluded to, and perhaps seems a little unlikely. The quote is included here for the record; readers can draw their own conclusions. The only other remarkable feature is that there is no suggestion relating to any of the tramways opened in the immediate period that the rolling stock was anything other than newly built for the individual line. There is however a remarkably close similarity between the design of the first London cars and cars used elsewhere, by comparison of the few remaining contemporary illustrations.

Copenhagen

The Copenhagen Railway Company was registered in London in June 1863 to construct and operate the first tramway in the Danish capital city, said to be the idea of a Dane, C F Tietgen, who had seen the London lines. The first section opened for traffic on 22 October 1863. The initial six cars, double-deck with nine-window saloons, appear from photographs as similar to Prentiss's cars built for Geneva, but have been credited as being the first built by George Starbuck.[155] This is not likely, nor is the suggestion that cars from Train's short-lived London ventures were used in Copenhagen.[156] It does, however, seem much more plausible that these vehicles could have been leased. A second batch of five cars — four double deck and one single deck — added by 1864 is said to have emanated from England, again most likely from Prentiss. In 1865, ten double deck cars were added, probably built in Philadelphia.[157] Other than Train's personal assertion, no evidence of his involvement has been determined. The initial horse tramway in Berlin (opened 22 June 1865) used cars built in Hamburg, copying those of Copenhagen.[158]

Top. Copenhagen, supposedly on the opening day of the horse tramway, 22 October 1863, at the Liberty Monument on Vesterbrogade. In 1904 the monument was moved to allow extension of the main railway station. The car is of the 'Birkenhead' nine window saloon style, but now improved with a spiral stair to access the top deck.

Pitt Street, Sydney, New South Wales

While obviously not a British tramway, the short line down Pitt Street, Sydney was equipped by Train with his patent rails and vehicles. From 1857 the Legislative Assembly of the Government of New South Wales, Australia, debated the desirability of connecting the terminus of the Western Railway at Redfern to the harbour area at Circular Quay by a 1¾ mile tramway down Pitt Street, for the carriage of goods and passengers. Three years later a contract for this was put out to tender in the UK and an offer from G F Train was accepted (through the Board of Trade) in January 1861 for supply of rails and two cars.[159] This appears to have been done prior to the necessary legislation receiving the assent of the State's Governor, which was achieved on 3 May 1861.[160] These were shipped on board the *Marcianus*, sailing from Liverpool on 27 April 1861. The cars were despatched 'in their complete state, the hatches of the vessel widened for their reception'.[161]

The vessel arrived after a stormy voyage of 89 days in Sydney on 26 July. The passage had been a rough one in more ways than one, with a great deal of animosity between crew and officers. Eight charges were laid when the ship docked, but the resentment took a serious turn when a deckhand assaulted the second mate during the unloading of the vessel. The mate, Edwin Brown died two days later and the deckhand responsible, George Kennedy, was charged with his murder.[162] The jury reduced this to manslaughter and Kennedy received a sentence of seven years hard labour.

Consternation followed when it was realised that the Train's rails were not, in fact, railway rails (necessary for the planned use of the line for railway wagons) but were his patent flat plates with upstand. The Government's Chief Engineer (Mr Whitton) was accused with having made a major error – and then of compounding the error by attempting to make the plate rails serve the purpose. They were described 'The rail is of iron plate, 5 inches wide, 1 inch depth, with a projection (on

Double deck horse tram built by Robert Main for Train's venture in Sydney NSW. Access to the top deck seats was by a vertical metal ladder and through a 'man-hole' opening in the canopy. The driver sat in an elevated position at the end of the top deck. This view on Pitt Street at Hunter Street shows this arrangement clearly. (Ken McCarthy collection)

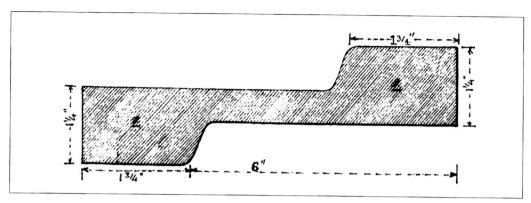

G F Train patented this design of reversible rail and employed it on the Sydney line. It was not successful there.

which the wheels will traverse) 1½ inch wide and ½ inch deep along the edge on one side, and the same on the opposite edge on the other side, so the rail is reversible at pleasure ... it appears that the flanges are to be turned so as to traverse the inner extremities of the rails ...'[163] Train's rails did not permit the passage of railway trucks (with deep flanges) which had been the major reason for construction of the line, and at Whitton's suggestion the rails were laid 'reversed' so that, to maintain the gauge at 4 ft 8½ ins, the plate part lay outside the track, rather than inside it. In addition, the tread of each wheel of the two new tramcars was machined down, thus increasing the depth of the flange by an equal amount. It was commented 'The object in making the flanges so small was not only that the corresponding shallow fall in the rails would cause the least possible interference of the roadway, but also that the cars might be got easily off the rails and restored to them, which is frequently necessary upon the street railways in England, and which it was doubtless supposed would be required on the Pitt-street tramway. It did not appear to be known by Mr Train, who provided the rails and cars, that the Tramway Act, passed by the Legislature last session, compelled all other vehicles to make way for the tramway cars, and that as, excepting these cars and the railway trucks, there would be no traffic on the line, it would never be necessary to lift the vehicles off the rails. In order to secure the car-wheels from slipping off the rails, they have been turned and a portion of the tire taken off, thereby increasing the depth of the flanges. Since these alterations have been made, the tramway has again been

tried, and the cars traversed and retraversed the line satisfactorily without once coming off the rails'.[164]

The most detailed report of the two vehicles is from the *Empire* newspaper '... the carriages, two in number ... resemble an omnibus, about double the length of a common one, but considerably wider. The seats, instead of being cross-wise, run the whole length of the carriage, one on each side. There is abundance of room to pass either up or down. On the roof there will also be seats, which will be reached by means of a steep iron ladder and a manhole. One of these elegant conveyances is capable of accommodating about sixty-three persons. The ladies will not, we imagine, be expected to sit on the roof; and if it were contemplated, it is questionable whether the present expensive style of dress would render so daring an achievement possible. Inside passengers can stand up without inconvenience, being at least seven feet high and very neatly designed. There are nine windows on each side and the sashes, which are neatly glazed, run in and out on slides. The internal fittings are really very neat and comfortable without being too costly. Suspended from the roof are a number of band straps, by means of which persons entering or leaving the coach may steady themselves without discommoding other passengers. Persons used to omnibus travelling will recognise this as an improvement. A leather strap runs directly under the roof from end to end of the carriage. The passenger who desires to get out, instead of wasting his breath in vain attempts to attract the attention of the driver, will simply give the strap a tug, and the result of this will be a most unmistakable tintinnabulation just over the head of that functionary. How such unwieldy articles as these carriages could have got into a ship's hold and out again, in good order, is surprising and reflects great credit on the master and crew of the *Marcianus*. Beyond a slight shake in one of the panels nothing could be in better order than the carriage inspected by us; as, indeed, the whole of the railway plant brought out by this vessel. The carriages are labelled 'Robert Main, Carriage Builder, Birkenhead, George Francis Train's Patent'".[165]

Several sources suggest that these cars accommodated 60 passengers, however the early photograph[166] of car 1 confirms a nine-window saloon which would probably indicate that the seating capacity was more likely 22 inside and the same on top with the total quoted probably including an allowance for standing passengers on the platforms. Access to the top deck was by vertical ladders leading through 'man-holes' formed in the canopy, on which there was a seat for the driver. 'The outside of the car has rather a gayish appearance, the body being a lively yellow; in the centre a lion, and an eagle taking the place of a unicorn being represented, with the motto, 'Unity is the strength of nations.' The names of the two cars are respectively '*Old England*' and '*Young Australia*.' There is a driving box at either end of the car, and on arriving at the Circular Quay the driver shifts this place and the pole, and the horses are transferred'.[167]

The line opened on 23 December, but criticism was already voiced about distortion of the newly sawn local ironbark (eucalyptus) timber used for longitudinal sleepers, plus severe buckling of the iron rails due to expansion in the summer heat. Considerable time and effort had already been expended to overcome these defects, but the result remained far from perfect and within six months suggestions were being made that the line should be abandoned. It was considered quite unsuitable for its main function, the transit of railway goods trucks to the quays, however in October 1862 this was this achieved.[168]

Horsing of the line was undertaken on contract by Alderman Woods, who took a three year lease of the operation of the line from the Government from 1

January 1864. That very month an accident resulted in the death of the elderly composer, 'Professor' Isaac Nathan,[169] and this has been wrongly cited as the reason for abandonment of operations. In fact this was but one of several accidents on the line, many to young boys indulging in the sporting habit of hanging on the cars for a free ride and a bit of fun – until the fall which frequently resulted in loss of part of a limb. The short line fulfilled a useful role, with a third car added in May 1864 (by which time the original two had lost their flamboyant names), this one built in Redfern railway workshops. It was described as being similar, but at 20 ft, two feet shorter than the first cars, with the outside seats 'laid on the projection that extends along the roof'. It cost £380 – compared to the delivered cost of £953.5.10d for the two English cars – which had then required further expenditure of £150 to prepare them.[170] This car was followed a year later by another, which replaced original car number 2. It has been suggested that damage had been caused to the cars on the rough voyage from England, probably accounting for the very short working life of this particular vehicle. After closure of the tramway the two locally built cars found further use on the Windsor to Richmond railway.[171]

The step rails in un-metalled roads caused the same problems as had been experienced elsewhere, and a Bill was introduced into the State Legislature for abandonment immediately upon expiry of Woods' lease. This was passed on 21 November 1866 and the tram operated finally on the last day of that year. The track was unceremoniously and immediately removed, work starting the following day.

A finely detailed and very well annotated article on the Pitt Street line in Sydney was prepared by Ken McCartney and published in the December 1981 issue of *Trolley Wire*, the journal of the Australian Tramway Museums. In this present work, reference has been made wherever possible to original sources, some of which have added detail not then available. For example, the builder of the first two tramway vehicles has been positively identified as Robert Main of Birkenhead.

Melbourne, Victoria

Train claimed in his dictated autobiography to have 'suggested' both railways in Victoria and street railways in Melbourne, the capital of the state.[172] As occasionally seen elsewhere, his prodigious memory was here playing him false – either consciously or subconsciously. He had arrived in Melbourne in May 1853 on the *Bavaria*, after a tedious 92-day journey from Boston, straight into what was then very much a 'frontier' town in the wildest days of the Great Australian gold-rush. Train, as agent for the White Star shipping line took advantage of the new colony's desperate need for imports of every variety and soon had a profitable enterprise under his control. He took fellow American George Starbuck as a partner from 1 November 1855, but then immediately left Australia after a hectic sojourn of just 2½ years. The enterprise was declared insolvent in September 1858, this possibly indicative of Starbuck's financial ineptitude (he went on to be declared bankrupt at least twice subsequently).

Francis Boardman Clapp was another Massachusetts born live-wire who arrived in Melbourne in 1853. His background in the USA had been in stage-coaches, and in Australia he was appointed agent for importation of the American 'Concord' coach. His experience led him into operation of up-country coach lines and by 1859 he was the largest contractor for mail coaching in Victoria. In May 1860 he, with five partners, formed a company and entered negotiations with Melbourne City Council for a horse tramway from the railway station in Spencer Street by Bourke Street to Collingwood. This was while the Sydney proposal was also under consideration, and just a few months after Train had arrived in England to commence his tramway adventures there. A lithograph illustrating his street tramway (probably the familiar one of Marble Arch) was sent by Train to Melbourne City Council in October 1860. The English proposals interested the Australian group and Clapp, despite in January 1861 having withdrawn his partnership, consulted Train in London.

The company appears to have agreed to obtain or to purchase two cars for the planned line in Melbourne, and probably made arrangements through Train. In 1861 Train was involved in a legal case instigated by Richard W Johnson, proprietor of the Railway Carriage and Wagon Co of Oldbury, for the cost of a tramcar built by Johnson and delivered to Train. It seems likely that this was part of the order which Train had given prematurely for cars to run on his planned line in Birmingham. One of these double-deck cars was exhibited in London during October 1860.

The *Maxwell* sailed from London on 29 April 1861. Mr Kent Hall (one of the promoters) advised '... the first instalment of rails and carriages are shipped in the Maxwell, the arrival of which is expected daily ...'[173] This was somewhat premature, as the ship was not to anchor at Melbourne until 12 August 1861. However all did not go according to plan, with the promoters having second thoughts regarding the 'ruinous' terms which they had agreed with the Council.

By mid 1861 enthusiasm had evaporated, but the two tramcars were now delivered. 'For five months past two of Train's patent carriages have been landed at the Hobson's Bay Railway station in Flinders street, and fittings for four more. It is not proposed, however, to have any other carriages imported, as it is estimated that they can be manufactured more cheaply in this colony. The delay caused to the company in laying down their ways has arisen from some legal difficulties in the agreement between them and the corporation. These are now likely to be adjusted in a week, and the company will then commence operations ...'[174] This does not reflect the reality of the situation, with the company no longer anxious to proceed.

That, however, was not quite the end of the venture. At the end of August 1878, the Argus carried an advertisement listing miscellaneous lots to be auctioned off at the Yarra-bank Works (being cleared as the property had been leased to the Government). Also known as 'William's Carriage Factory at Batman's Swamp', the facility had constructed railway rolling stock since c.1862, owned by William Williams – one of the original partners of the tramway company. The lots to be sold on 5 September included 2 street tramway cars, spare tram wheels, bent and other timbers, etc.[175] What became of these two vehicles is unknown – having been unused for over fifteen years, the likelihood is that the boring insects of Australia would have reduced much to sawdust.

F B Clapp was deeply involved with urban transport for his entire career, finally as Chairman of the Melbourne Tramway and Omnibus Coy.

The details of this abortive Australian tramway proposal have been provided by Brian Weedon, to whom particular thanks is recorded.

Darlington

One of Train's provincial endeavours was in Darlington, where he had been initially approached by Mr John E MacNay (later to become Chief Cashier of the North Eastern Railway) who enlisted the influential Quaker Pease family to the cause. Proposals were submitted to the meeting of the local Board of Health on 7 November 1861. Just four days later, (and before any plans had been approved) applications were solicited for shares in the Darlington Street Railway Company (Limited), 600 shares of £5 each providing a working capital of

£3000, very soon increased to £4000. Henry Pease M. P. of Pierremont was appointed Chairman of the company which, no doubt as a consequence of the positive influence of heavyweight local involvement, immediately placed contracts for two cars from Prentiss of Birkenhead, and for rails from Barningham's Albert Hill Ironworks in Darlington (where Henry Pease also happened to be Chairman). Another contract, for construction of the line, was promptly negotiated with Charles Hathaway. Such was the degree of confidence that this all took place prior to official approval, which was recorded at the Board of Health's meeting of 5 December 1861. 'The application for leave to lay down a Street Railway from the East end of Blackwellgate to the East end of Whessoe-street, having been considered '... the Board will not offer any objection thereto, the parties concerned having expressed their willingness to take up the rails and restore the road to its original state at the end of three years, if the same, or the working of the railroad, should prove to be a public nuisance, and the company guaranteeing that the same shall be worked with as little interruption to the ordinary traffic as the nature of the line will admit, and saving this Board harmless in respect thereto.'[176]

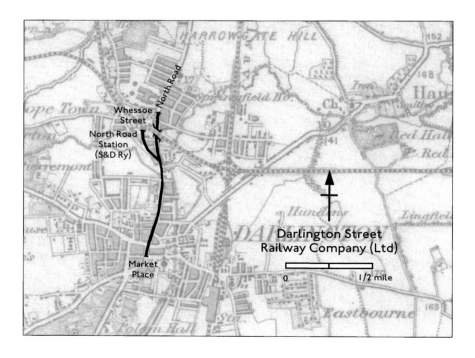

The two cars, patriotically named '*Wellington*' and '*Nelson*', were delivered by the middle of December, and then stored in the new engine shops of the Stockton & Darlington Railway in Durham Road. The five inch wide plate rails described appear to be a variant on those in use on earlier lines, with the width in two strips, one two inches wide level with the road surface, the other, three inches wide, inside and ½ inch below this. Operation around sharp curves was described '... The wheels of the car are only six feet apart, so that a curve can be worked having a radius of thirty-three feet. On the inside of the curve a gutter [grooved] rail is fixed, and on the outside is a flat piece of iron, instead of a rail, which, on the car turning, gives a play to the wheels. The cars are also constructed on a particular patented plan, which admits of their working easily on curves ... when viewed from a distance, Nelson looked like one of Wombwell's caravans.'[177] [George Wombwell was then well known for his 'Travelling Menagerie' which toured the country with animals in a dozen or so caravans.]

Construction started immediately and was quickly completed, the route of just ¾ mile from the Market Place to North Road railway station sufficiently advanced to allow a trial run to be arranged for 26 December 1861. Unfortunately this was interrupted by several derailments at the junction of the branch to the railway station, where necessary adjustments were immediately put in hand.

A formal opening ceremony on 1 January was described in fine detail 'Precisely at nine o'clock in the morning, the first car started from the Workman's Institute, driven by Frank Thompson ... well known as the person who had the honour some years ago of driving the first cab in this town ... The 'Nelson' was the first car that arrived, and the 'Wellington' presently after followed ... they run along so pleasantly that one might almost imagine one's self on the bosom of an unruffled lake ... occasionally there was a jerk, caused by the wheels passing over a stone, but such defects are easily remediable ... A driver from the Birkenhead street railway had charge of the horses in the second

Rather indistinct, but this is the only known view recording Train's short-lived tramway in Darlington. One of the two cars stands near the southern terminus on Prebend Row. The line was given permission to operate for three years only, after which the tramway was closed. (Courtesy of the Centre for Local Studies, Darlington)

car, and the dexterity with which he handled his beasts and applied the brake so as to avoid running off the curves was admirable; still, not a few preferred Frank's driving. The very fact of the cars keeping on the rails proves the ability of both in this respect. The conductors were dressed in their uniforms, which are remarkably tasty, and made of excellent material.'[178] A 'splendid breakfast' was enjoyed after the event, held in the old goods station of the Stockton and Darlington Railway.[179] The assembled guests were subjected to the by now fully anticipated harangue from Mr Train, who had journeyed north to join the opening junket. He could not resist the opportunity to respond to the highly charged words which had been used against him in recent press diatribes '… He wished to thank the people of Darlington for his courteous reception … their gentlemanly courtesy was entirely different to what he had received elsewhere. He had been in various towns and places, and spent his money and brain for the good of the community, but he had been misrepresented everywhere. Here, however, he had been treated as a gentleman. He came to this country, and at his own expense and with vast labour had succeeded in introducing his idea, but notwithstanding all his good intentions a large combination had risen against him, vilified him in the public prints, and mis-represented everything he had done and said. He wanted the people of Darlington to understand him better. He then referred to his recent conduct in the respect to the dispute between this country and America, and said that because he loved his country better than this he had been set down as a hypocrite and traitor … notwithstanding the persecution he had met with he should remain among them until he was sent out of the country, considering that in doing so he had as perfect a right as the millions of Englishmen who were scattered over the American continent, had a right to stay there."[180]

Two weekly broadsheets covered local events, the 'Darlington Telegraph', which was anti the Pease's and their enterprises, hence carried all the news which could reflect against them, and the 'Darlington and Stockton Times', which tended to present a more balanced view. Every incident was elaborated by the 'Telegraph' in florid language; on one occasion a derailment just by the Railway Tavern; 'There was a fearful rush of passengers higgledy-piggledy, caulk-ow'er-keel, neck-or-nothing, rumble-tumble, hurry-scurry out of great Nelson's body' described the scene graphically. However in September 1863 an event took place which possibly aided the demise of the line. A pedigree – and potentially profitable – greyhound belonging to local auctioneer Charles Miller was killed by one of the trams. £50 in compensation was demanded – equivalent then to the annual wage of a working man. 'There was plenty of time to stop if the driver had been inclined, but being a man of rare astuteness, he merely put his whistle to his mouth and blew, which, however it might have alarmed a Christian, had no effect upon the dog, which, failing to see the urgent necessity for moving, was run over and its forelegs broken'. Miller pursued the Company's Directors personally, but came unstuck at the Crown Court when he was advised that his claim should be against the Company and the judge entered the case as 'nonsuit', or withdrawn due to lack of evidence.[181] Miller persisted and took his plea to London, whence it was promptly returned to the Durham Assizes; but subsequent events overtook his action, the company being dissolved before any outcome.

Local traders were vociferous in their criticisms of the obstruction caused by the position of the line, and many complaints were made, and difficulties created to operation of the cars by merchandise being deliberately unloaded on top of the track. These eventually resulted in a motion being put before the Local Board of Health that the tramways' tenure be ended. On 7 July 1864 the Board passed a motion (by just one vote) that notice be given that the street railway be removed at the end of the current year, and the road fully restored. However as several members of the Board were shareholders in the Company, opinion of Counsel was sought, eventually determining (in November) that they were not entitled to vote on this motion.[182]

There were, however, supporters of the tramway, and a petition signed by some 600 local inhabitants, submitted 'We desire to express to you our unanimous belief that notwithstanding that at the outset the undertaking was opposed, and disparaged by a few, it is now regarded by a large majority of the people as a great public convenience, a readily available, comfortable, and cheap mode of conveyance, and one which ought not to be done away with on the representations merely of a very limited minority, who may have yielded to feelings of prejudice. We therefore urge upon you most respectfully but most earnestly to take into consideration the excellent accommodation it has afforded to the multitude, and especially to the humbler classes of society, when upwards of 40,000 passengers per annum have been carried during the two years of its existence, and trust you will reconsider and rescind the resolution ...'.[183] The gainsayers quickly responded that a memorial by 600, from a population of 16,000 was significant, and some of these signatures could be from shop-boys, and others of maid-servants!

The tramway's unpopularity with the town's traders and assorted cattle dealers and farmers was sufficient to promote a counter attack, but this attracted only 225 signatures. '... The tramway is found to be specially an inconvenience and source of danger in connection with the horse fair, now yearly becoming of greater importance, and seriously interferes with the exhibition of stock'.[184] Its presence was particularly resented on market days, when previously traders had uninterrupted use of the streets.

Not long before the authorised three year period of operation expired, a shareholders' meeting decided to apply for an extension of the licence. The meeting to determine this was eventually held on 23 December. The chairman of the Local Board of Health (Mr Joseph Pease), noting that the line was used by 'sometimes so many as 1000 persons ... in a week", was happy for the line to remain. Voting was 7 for the motion to allow the line to continue, 5 for the amendment. The Clerk to the Board then advised that as there was not a majority of the 15 members present, neither motion nor amendment was carried and that the resolution of 7 July must prevail.[185] Despite being popular with many, the line was never profitable, losing

£77 in the first year of operation and £110 in the second.[186]

The cars ceased operating on Saturday night, 31 December 1864 with a three-horse bus obtained from Manchester and run by Mr J Wetherell taking their place. The Street Railway Company was instructed to remove the plate rails as soon as possible, if possible before the next Horse Show; they were lifted during February. Even the 'Telegraph' was forced to concede 'It cannot be denied that the cars were a great convenience to thousands [who will miss] the great rumbling, clanging car, with light flaming and reflected from its bright yellow front, making night jaundiced with its colour and hideous with its din.'[187] The company was placed into voluntary liquidation on 31 January 1866, investors receiving about 4 shillings in the pound for their shares. The rails were immediately lifted and the cars sold, their subsequent fate unrecorded.[188]

Staffordshire Potteries

Other than Birkenhead, the only other of Train's first generation tramways to have an extended life (both as a consequence of an early change to grooved rail) was that promoted as the Staffordshire Potteries Street Railway Company Limited. In the Potteries towns the prospect of a tramway to Train's patent was eagerly solicited, particularly by Mr Joseph S Forbes, Borough Surveyor of Hanley. Soon after Train commenced his crusade for adoption of his patented street railways into the United Kingdom, he was approached by Forbes, who considered that the Potteries area was so badly served by public transport that a line should be laid commencing in Longton, then by Fenton, Hanley, Burslem and Tunstall, to end in Goldenhill – a distance of over seven miles.

Train first visited the area in early October 1861, a trip which was quickly followed by all relevant local Road's Boards declaring in favour of his proposal. This result probably resulted more from Forbes' efforts than those of Train, who bluntly declared that he had not come into the area as a philanthropist, but to make

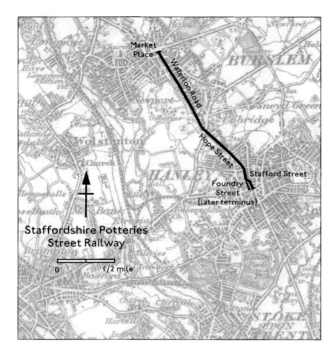

Staffordshire Potteries
Street Railway

Plan of Burslem
terminus

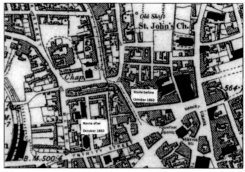

Plan of
Hanley
terminus

money! He felt confident of achieving this if his scheme was carried out, and quoted figures relating to the Surrey Side line. Here he said 3000 passengers per day were being carried and that in seven weeks of operation takings were £1200 against costs of £500. A return of £100 a week was being achieved against a total outlay of £5000. Relative to the proposed Potteries line he was so convinced of its potential that he was prepared to fund it himself, but nevertheless would prefer that a local company be formed so that people of the neighbourhood could invest in the scheme, also he considered that the line would be more popular if local people had a pecuniary interest in its wellbeing.[189]

At a meeting on 28 November 1861 it was resolved to enter an agreement with Train for a line to link Burslem to Hanley 'the exact termini to be hereafter agreed'. This was to be complete and ready for traffic on 1st January 1862, at a cost of £2500 per mile – £2000 for construction and £500 to Train for royalty. [At this period, a school teacher's salary could be £50 per annum] £500 was to be paid in cash when the work was half complete, and one quarter of the total value of the contract was to be taken by Train in fully paid–up shares.[190]

Within a month the Staffordshire Potteries Street Railway Company (Limited) was formed, and negations were well under way, with Hathaway undertaking to construct at the rate of one mile of track per week. However the citizenry were slow to subscribe, so a decision was taken to proceed initially with the 'branch' line from Hanley to Burslem. The nominal capital of the new company amounted to £20,000 in 4000 shares of £5 each. Of these just 1341 were taken up, there being only 93 individual shareholders[191]. 'The curiosity of those desirous of seeing the kind of vehicle which will run along the street railway will be gratified in a day or two by an opportunity of inspecting one of the cars which will be sent down for that purpose'.[192] This indeed came to pass, with a report less than a week later 'On Monday morning one of the cars to be used on the Burslem and Hanley branch of the Potteries Street railway arrived at Stoke station by train from Birkenhead. In the course of the afternoon it was drawn to Hanley attended by a crowd of admirers … to the Market Square, where it was located for a time for exhibition. Yesterday it was taken to Burslem [and] is to be exhibited in the other towns in the district. The car is of the largest size calculated to carry about forty passengers, inside and on the roof, and is altogether very handsome as well as commodious … the car is named '*Justice*'.[193] The photograph does not appear to show that '*Justice*' then carried top deck passengers.

Perhaps the principle of a street tramway had been accepted readily in Burslem as the town had already seen a similar such innovation years earlier. When the Trent and Mersey Canal was constructed in the first decade of the nineteenth century a ½ mile branch took it to Burslem Wharf. From the wharf a horse drawn mineral tramway was laid along the centre of Navigation Road, to carry the canal's merchandise the final distance – about another ½ mile up to the Market Square. This line is shown on Hargreaves' 1832 map of the Potteries, but had gone by the time of the survey for the 1851 Ordnance plan.

Construction of the 1¾ mile long line was undertaken with alacrity, work commencing at the 'Blue Bell' on Waterloo Road on 4 December 1861 with completion achieved (except the final 200 yards in Burslem) on 11 January following. An opening ceremony took place just two days later, on 13 January 1862. On that day both cars, laden with local dignitaries, started from Hanley, travelled without incident to Burslem, then returned to Hanley Town Hall where 'refreshments awaited'. G F Train was unavoidably detained elsewhere, but his health was drunk in absentia. The cars ran every half hour, thirteen times per day, leaving both termini at the same time and passing at the mid-point; the fare being 3d each way. Unfortunately this relatively high fare was necessary as tolls amounting to 26/- per day were imposed by the turnpike road authority (1/- each time a tram passed Cobridge Toll.) Sunday operation was provided from the start, but with only three return trips.

The company held its first annual meeting in Hanley Town Hall on 31 January, and it is apparent that the organisation was already looking to the future. Although the initial length of track had been in use for a very short period, extension both north and south was deemed a necessity, and it was calculated that if the level of traffic so far enjoyed held up, then a return of 7% on capital was likely. Expenditure recorded included

£479.15s for two cars [*Justice* and *Queen*] and their delivery costs, seven horses and keep prior to the opening £170, harness and uniforms £43 5s 9d, alterations to office and stables £48 10s 9d etc. Local youths had fun placing stones on the rails to be crushed by (or to derail) the passing tram, but their excitement was severely dampened when two miscreants were taken before the local magistrate, and for their 'fun' were fined 10/- each – with the alternative of 28 days in prison![194]

An extraordinary meeting held at the beginning of October 1862 the directors decided to 'improve the existing line' in order to make it less inconvenient to other traffic on the roadway. Two court cases had resulted from damage said to have been occasioned by the step rail, with costs against the company of almost £700. The Chairman (Mr Baker) considered that '… unless they could put down a different rail every penny which had been invested in the company would be thrown away, and being fully satisfied of the efficacy of a grooved rail, although it had been pronounced against by some practical men, he induced the directors to lay down a short length of the grooved design of rail, and this being successful it was laid it over the total length. The new rail answered very satisfactorily, for while before it was adopted there was not a single week in which there were no complaints, and calls for compensation for accidents, there had not been since a single complaint, and not a couple of pounds paid. This new rail had cost them their dividend, but it had been the means of saving, not only that, but other street railways. No sooner had the groove principle been successfully tested in this district than it was adopted on the Birkenhead Street Railway, with the result that, a year ago a Judge and Jury at Chester decided that the line was not a nuisance to the public, but a convenience. To avoid such continuing problems reconstruction using grooved rail was intended.'[195]

At the second annual meeting at the beginning of February 1863, a dividend was declared, but at a more realistic level of 2½ %. This, it was stated, would have been greater but for one-off charges incurred in setting up the company – mostly payments to Train and Hathaway. However, and more significantly, it was

Top. Fine view of the car '*Justice*'. This car is similar to several of the cars illustrated earlier. Probably taken at the Foundry Street terminus, Hanley. (Courtesy of Stoke-on Trent Museums)

Above. The other car which, with '*Justice*' formed the entire initial fleet, was '*Queen*'. It carries a fleet number – 15 – on the dash, which may possibly relate to a local authority licence.

announced that it was the intention in the coming spring [of 1863] to move the track from Burslem south as far as Cobridge (almost half the total length of the line) from the centre of the highway to the side of the road – and to introduce the new grooved rail while this was done. The superintendent of the line, Mr Hodginson, was to add the role of company secretary to his other duties. In the twelve months that the line had operated some 152,290 fare paying passengers had been conveyed, considered a satisfactory result in a period of industrial depression.[196]

Hanley Town Council at a meeting early in September 1863 gave their permission to relay the line within the town with a new rail, and also agreed that the line could be diverted from Stafford Street to Foundry Street to avoid a very awkward curve at the top of Hope Street.[197] Work began immediately, and was completed in mid October. For some reason (perhaps a sufficient supply of the new rail was not to hand) the work was done, in the wider part of Foundry Street in the old rail, and with the new rail only in the narrow part. The new terminus was at Trinity Street. At the other end of the line the old rails were removed from alongside Burslem Town Hall, but when construction of the new track in the centre of the street was commenced, the market traders objected, so a new terminus was created a few yards further south.[198]

The third annual report, while acknowledging the lack of any dividend, indicated that all surplus cash had been utilised in execution of improvements to the line.[199] By the end of 1864 the line had been entirely re-laid, the following year celebrated by successful operation with not a single accident and not a single complaint. A third car was purchased that year at a cost of £133. This probably came from Prentiss (or Starbuck) in Birkenhead, but this has not been confirmed. The line was leased to George Bradford for five years from March 1864, and following the addition of the third car, his annual rent was increased from £300 to £315. The short line established a regular pattern of successful operation and by 1867 returned a dividend of 4% to the shareholders, increased to 5% for the following year.

Mr Benjamin Boothroyd, a Director of the company was called before the House of Commons Select Committee on the Tramways Bill in 1870; some of his statements give insight into working the line not otherwise available.[200] At this time, he stated, the line while carrying some 200,000 passengers per annum, was not a profitable speculation. Although leased out, a composition toll was still being paid to the turnpike road trustees. Also 'We originally put down the American rail, the flat rail, but we found that dangerous owing to accidents, and we devised a rail of our own, a grooved rail, and substituted that for our rail; one is grooved and one is flat. ... [the line] is not paved, it is macadamised ... [laid] upon the ground ... We were unfortunate in that matter [the cost of construction]. I think the actual cost of the undertaking would not have been above £1500 or £1600 a mile, and the stocking of it was perhaps about £1000 more; but we fell into bad hands. We gave a concession of £500 a mile to Mr Train for a presumed royalty, and I think we were indeed cheated in the experiment by the constructor, who was an American also. It could have been put down for £1500 a mile. It was put down contract. The capital of our two miles now, including everything, is £6000". We also confirm from this exchange an insight into Train's dealings; he demanded a royalty, presumably for the use of his 'patented' rail – no doubt this was also extracted from his other lines.

At the sixteenth Annual Meeting in February 1877, it was noted that '... nothing has been expended on the cars in the course of the last year but it is regretted to say that they are showing signs of breaking up. The directors are negotiating for the purchase of two good and serviceable cars at a very reasonable rate ...' During the following year a new car was added (at a cost of £170) then, at the end of 1879, the original company was sold to the newly formed North Staffordshire Tramways Company Ltd.

This, despite Mr Boothroyd's doubts, was possibly the most successful of Train's lines. It was immortalised in Arnold Bennett's 'The Old Wives' Tale', which – to judge by his other writings on the five towns is a fair reflection of how life was then lived out. [For Bursley read Burslem and for Handbridge read Hanley.] 'Incredible as it may appear, there was nothing but a horse tram running between Bursley and Handbridge – and that only twice an hour; and between the other towns no stage of any kind! One went to Longshaw as one now goes to Peking. A poor, blind, complacent people! The ludicrous horse-car was typical of then. The driver rang a huge bell, five minutes before the starting, that could be heard from the Wesleyan Chapel to the Cock Yard and then after deliberations and hesitation the vehicle rolled off on its rails into unknown dangers while passengers shouted good-bye. And this was regarded as the last word of traction.'[201]

The Staffordshire Potteries Street Railway does demand a place in British tramway history as the first to appreciate, and to put into effect, the change from step to grooved rail, and thus set the pattern for successful future development of the 'street railway' philosophy in the United Kingdom. What was probably Train's final tramway proposal was made in February 1862. A new road was proposed by the Metropolitan Board of Works to cross Hyde Park from Kensington to Bayswater. Train proposed that, when the road was constructed, he would lay a tramway, offering a toll of one farthing per passenger, or a lump sum of £2000. This was insufficient to tempt the Board; no tramway resulted.[202] Train returned to North America in October 1862[203] – he never again visited England. A measure of his unpopularity can be gauged from the report of 'an immense effigy of Tramway Train, wearing a fool's cap, was ... carried through London in a cart pulled by two donkeys.[204]

Some years later Train's actions caught up with him. On a visit to Ireland in January 1868, ostensibly to visit Cork and Dublin on street railway matters, he was immediately arrested; his Fenian sympathies apparently sufficient to justify this action.[205] After a few days incarcerated in Cork jail he moved on to Dublin, only to be re-arrested, this time as a debtor. 'The public have received with remarkable indifference the news of Mr G. F. Train's consignment to the limbo of insolvent debtors, but he is not without admirers of a certain class ... He has been arrested on a judge's fiat for a debt of

£800 alleged due to the Ebbw Vale Iron Co for rails supplied in 1861 to the London Tramways Co. Train insisted that the debt had been paid long since 'or, if not, that the Bank of England and some eminent English firms are as responsible for it as I am''[206]. A completely unbowed Train was immediately consigned to Dublin's Marshalsea Prison for debtors where he languished for nearly ten months until released in December. While it was claimed that the debt and associated costs had been paid, Train absolutely denied this, but he wasted no time before promptly returning to the United States. He never ventured eastward across the Atlantic again, and always maintained his complete blamelessness.

Some thirty years later Train was interviewed by the *Street Railway Review*, and recorded some memories of his time promoting the English lines:

'I was surprised to find that ... there were no street railways in the Old World.

It seems to have been my destiny to introduce on land and sea in foreign lands, new inventions promoting trade and commerce everywhere!

Easton, Charles Hathaway, Saunders (my contractors) were pioneers in the business when I launched my first 'tramway' (as the English call it), abroad, at Birkenhead, opposite Liverpool, England! John Laird, builder of the 'Alabama' (Blockade Pirate), gave me contract: (I taking all risks and agreeing to remove it if failure!)

That road was opened August 1859 [sic] and extended to adjoining towns ... John Stephenson (the great Car Builder, still alive) sent me first car (in shooks) from shops opposite where I am writing this ... My first London Road was from Marble Arch (Hyde Park) to Bogswater! [sic] next from Victoria Station to Westminster Abbey and Parliament House! Third from Westminster Bridge to Kensington [sic] Gate! Each line, (with lines promised in all leading parishes)!

inaugurated with Banquets ... My patents were made fast all over World and America ... I was the most popular American abroad. My patents (as promoter and patentee) can not be outlawed. Three hundred million dollars now are invested in street railways in England and my royalty will amount to $15,000,000.) ... [207]

The journal quoted above, on page 469, quotes Hathaway as saying that the first vehicles for the English street railway were made in Philadelphia and erected in England by him. On the very next page Train states that the [same] cars were built for him by John Stephenson! Contemporary references all give credit to Robert Main – which is where all trust-worthy evidence points. As late as March 1875 Train still considered that his English enterprises owed him a fortune; listed then among his assets was a claim for $1 million against the 'Home Railroad Co of Birkenhead County, England'. At that time, it is said he owned only the clothes on his back.[208]

Train died on 5 January 1904, having dictated his autobiography – entirely from memory, and without reference to diaries or notes – over several weeks in July and August 1902. As can be appreciated from the above, it seems more than likely that his memory was playing him false in some details; perhaps not to be wondered at when his life's achievements are weighed. In the Preface even he had to acknowledge this '... I beg my readers to remember that this book was spoken, not written, by me. ... It may not, in every part, agree with the recollections of others; but I am sure that it is as accurate in statement as it is blameless in purpose. If I should fail at any point, this will be due to some wavering of memory, and not to intention. Thanks to my early Methodist training, I have never knowingly told a lie; and I shall not begin at this time of life'.[209] Train had a prodigious memory – indeed after his death his brain was compared to the average,

and found to weigh 53.8 ounces; no less than 12 % larger than average.[210] His brain was preserved in the specimen collection of Dr Edward Anthony Spitzka of the Association of American Anatomists' Committee on Brain Bequests. Spitzka found it, not just larger than average, but remarkable for the 'structural features [which are] admirable in the depth and complexity of the fissures and convolutions with which it is marked.'[211]

George Francis Train was a unique and quite remarkable man who achieved a great deal, and regarding whom most subsequent historians have felt content to follow earlier writings. However, by reference to as many contemporary accounts as can be located, perhaps a fuller and more accurate eulogy may now have been recorded.

Conclusion

Train's objective was undoubtedly to make money for himself. His costs needed to be absorbed by the capital of any new operating organisation, which would have had absolutely no experience of what 'reasonable' costs should amount to. The USA was then rife with over-capitalisation which was a major factor in the subsequent collapse of the street railway industry in the 1920s when it the true costs of maintaining businesses became clearer – the other major contributory factor, of course, being the rise of the automotive industry and the affordability of mass-produced automobiles. Were Train's costs higher than equivalents outside US practice? Did he contribute to an American myth that urban tramways were or could be 'goldmines'? Some questions still remain to be answered. However it must be said that the flamboyant American left behind him, following his brief sojourn in the British Isles, a turmoil of opinion weighed heavily against his patented design of street railway construction. This was to take the best part of a decade to overcome.

Train's trams

Line	Number/Name	Builder	Date	Type	Seating
Bd	No 1	Robert Main	1860	d/d	22/22
Bd	No 2	Robert Main	1860	d/d	22/22
Bd	No 3	Robert Main	1860	s/d	0/22
Bd	No 4	Robert Main	1860	s/d	0/22
Sy	OLD ENGLAND	Robert Main	1861	d/d	22/22?
Sy	NEW AUSTRALIA	Robert Main	1861	d/d	22/22?
MA	HER MAJESTY	Kimball & Gorton	1861	s/d	0/24
MA	PRINCE CONSORT	Kimball & Gorton	1861	s/d	0/24
MA	PRINCESS ROYAL	Kimball & Gorton	1861	s/d	0/24
VS	THE PEOPLE	Kimball & Gorton?	1861	s/d	0/24
VS	?	Railway Carriage Co Ltd	1860	d/d	22/18
SS	THE ARMY	Kimball & Gorton?	1861	s/d	
SS	THE NAVY	Kimball & Gorton?	1861	s/d	
SS	HOPE	Kimball & Gorton?	1861	s/d	
SS	[CHARITY]?	Kimball & Gorton?	1861	s/d	
Bd	VICTORIA	Kimball & Gorton?	1861	s/d	
Bd	[ALBERT]?	Kimball & Gorton?	1861	s/d	
Bd	YOUNG ENGLAND	Stephenson?	1861	s/d★	
Bd	YOUNG AMERICA	Stephenson?	1861	s/d★	
Bd	MAY QUEEN	Stephenson?	1861	s/d	
Dtn	NELSON	E F Prentiss	1861	s/d	0/22
Dtn	WELLINGTON	E F Prentiss	1861	s/d	0/22
SP	JUSTICE	E F Prentiss	1861	s/d	
SP	QUEEN	E F Prentiss	1861	s/d	

Abbreviations:

Bd, Birkenhead; MA, Marble Arch; VS, Victoria Street; SS, Surrey Side; Sy, Sydney; Dtn, Darlington; SP, Staffordshire Potteries.
s/d, single deck; d/d, double deck

Other vehicles may have existed, as *four* cars are recorded being used on the Marble Arch line – unless cars were moved around from line to line as required. It is not impossible that the cars employed on the tramways at Darlington and the Potteries had seen previous use on the London lines, but all contemporary press reports appear to indicate that these cars were newly constructed.

★ 'YOUNG AMERICA' was involved in an accident in September 1861, when it was also referred to as No 8 car. 'YOUNG ENGLAND' was advertised for sale from Starbuck's in 1886 'where it has lain for many years'. Several cars for the Birkenhead line were imported from America in 1861. 'A firm in Philadelphia have just finished a railroad car for the Birkenhead Street Railway … similar to those built for the roads in Philadel-

Street Railway buckle and button, probably the design used on Train's three London tramways. (Collection of Ashley Birch)

phia. The weight of the car is 3575 lbs and its cost about $900. The builders of the car intend to put in estimates for all the cars to be run on the English passenger roads.'[212] As one of these is known to have been named 'VICTORIA', another must surely have been 'ALBERT' (who died quite unexpectedly on 14 December 1861). Another Birkenhead car, which was also referred to as No 9, was named 'MAY QUEEN' and was in use by August 1862. The logical companion for 'HOPE' would be 'CHARITY' – or perhaps 'FAITH' – but while the first has contemporary reference, no other name has yet been uncovered.

Reporting on the Bayswater Road line opening, the *Morning Star* stated '... the next cars building by Messers E. F. Prentiss are the EARL OF LONSDALE, THE PRESS, THE PEOPLE, etc; other cars to be called the PRINCE OF WALES, PRINCE ALBERT etc are in course of construction by Mr R. W. Johnson at Birmingham ...' This would tend to confirm that cars imported from the USA did indeed pass through Prentiss's Birkenhead workshops.

Early tramway cars were brightly painted – and most were named – in the same manner as most contemporary horse omnibuses. In Birkenhead the waist and dash were pale green, the Bayswater cars were 'lemon chrome'; for Victoria Street they were probably pale blue (if the model in London's Science Museum collection is considered an accurate representation), the Potteries cars may have been cream, the Darlington cars were yellow; the Sydney cars described as 'bright

yellow'. No detail has yet been discovered for the livery of cars on the Surrey Side line.

The first tramway in Geneva (opened 19 June 1862) used double-deck vehicles, the initial six cars being built in Birkenhead by Prentiss.[213] It has been also postulated that the first six cars for the Copenhagen tramway (opened 22 October 1863) may have been previously used on Train's London lines; this is not likely. Prentiss probably constructed the first Copenhagen cars, and possibly also the initial cars for Buenos Aires.

Prentiss provided details of his cars for Darlington; 'The car is 20 feet long, 7 feet in height inside, with a clear space of 3½ feet between the seats, which run along both sides as in a saloon railway carriage. At each end are projecting eaves; and platforms for the conductor and driver to stand upon, each of which are capable of accommodating three or four passengers with room to stand. The body of the car, which is on a level with the platforms, is only 18 inches from the ground. At each side of the end platforms are two steps for getting up and down. The entrances are at both ends from the platforms, through sliding doors. The sides of the car are furnished with glass windows, having sun shades. There is a strap running along the roof of the car, which communicates at each end with a bell, so that a passenger can at any time pass the order to both conductor and driver that he or she wishes to alight. At dark, the car is illuminated inside by gas from a lamp in the centre of the roof, and on the outside over the platforms, at each end are red signal lamps. The inside fittings are on a similar comfortable scale to those of a first-class railway carriage. Each car runs according to a time table, and is furnished with a clock. The 3½ feet space between the seats and the height (7 feet) admit of easy ingress and egress, without interfering with ladies' crinolines or gentlemen's legs. Each car has sitting room for 22 passengers, and standing room outside on the platforms for 8 more, while some cars are built to carry 22 additional passengers on the roof. A Street Railway Car only weighs 3,300 pounds, and, from its lightness, can with ease attain a speed of ten miles an hour. Its speed, which it partly owes to its lightness and undeviating course, allows of a greater number of trips being made in a day than with an omnibus: this and its capacity for carrying a larger number of passengers, admits of cheaper fares being remunerative. The horses are attached by a self-supporting pole, fastened to the car by a pin, and therefore can be transferred in a moment to either end, which is necessary, as the car does not turn, but runs sometimes with one end forward, and sometimes the other.'[214]

Train frequently alluded to himself as 'Young America', for example in autobiographical books *Young America Abroad* (1857) and *Young America in Wall Street* (1858). The phrase however was also used as a generalisation to symbolise the dynamic spirit of the new young republic and its go-getting style of enthusiastic expansionism. Train was seen by some – and probably himself – as 'Young America' incarnate. He was also regularly referred to as 'Citizen Train'.

Other Contemporary Tramway Vehicles in England

Line	Name	Builder	Date	Type	Seating	
VS	?	Railway Carriage Coy [Oldbury]	1861	d/d	22/18?	★

★ Several street railway carriages were ordered in 1860 and 1861 from this company, a number (two?) were built to Train's instruction for his projected (but never constructed) street railway for Birmingham, then possibly further four commenced for his London lines. Only one is known to have been used, on the Victoria Street line; those completed for Birmingham were possibly sent to Melbourne, but never used.

MA+SS	ENTERPRISE	Robert Main	1861	d/d	16/20	★★

★★ Built to William Curtis's Patent, with removable flanges on front wheels; operated in Liverpool then briefly in London in opposition to Train's vehicles.

Bd	OLD ENGLAND	Robert Main	1862	s/d	0/22?	★★★
Bd	LOOK-OUT	Robert Main	1862	s/d	0/22?	★★★

★★★ Built for Thomas Evans to operate on the Birkenhead line; 'similar to those already running'.

Chronology of G F Train's Tramway Activities 1859–1866

16 January 1859	Arrives in Liverpool on ss *Asia*
3 February 1860	Initial approach to Liverpool Dock Board Works Committee
9 March 1860	Initial approach to Birkenhead Commissioners
1 July 1860	Work commences at Birkenhead
5 July 1860	Initial approach to Glasgow Police Committee
17 July 1860	GF Train letter to Wednesbury Turnpike Trustees re tramway
9 August 1860	Initial letter to Westminster District Board of Works
30 August 1860	Opening of Birkenhead Street Railway
5 October 1860	Initial approach to Edinburgh Council Roads Board
8 November 1860	GF Train initial appearance before vestry of Lambeth
23 March 1861	Opening of Bayswater tramway (Marble Arch Street Rail Co Ltd)
15 April 1861	Opening of Victoria Street tramway (Westminster Street Rail Co Ltd)
19 June 1861	GF Train letter to Sir James Shelley
15 August 1861	Opening of the Surrey Side tramway (Surrey Side Street Rail Co Ltd)
c19 September 1861	Closure of Bayswater tramway
23 December 1861	Opening of Sydney (NSW) tramway
1 January 1862	Opening of Darlington tramway
13 January 1862	Opening of Staffordshire Potteries tramway
6 March 1862	Closure of Victoria Street tramway
19 June 1862	Opening of Burn's Geneva tramway
21 June 1862	Closure of Surrey Side tramway
20 August 1862	GF Train leaves for Newfoundland on ss *Mavrockadatis* [Spelling as in note (1); correct spelling is *Mavrocordatos*]
14 July 1863	Opening of Buenos Aires tramway (No Train connection established)
8 September 1863	Opening of St Petersburg tramway (No Train connection established)
22 October 1863	Opening of Copenhagen Railway Company (tramway)
25 June 1864	Opening of Den Haag to Scheveningen tramway
31 December 1864	Closure of Darlington tramway
31 December 1866	Closure of Sydney tramway

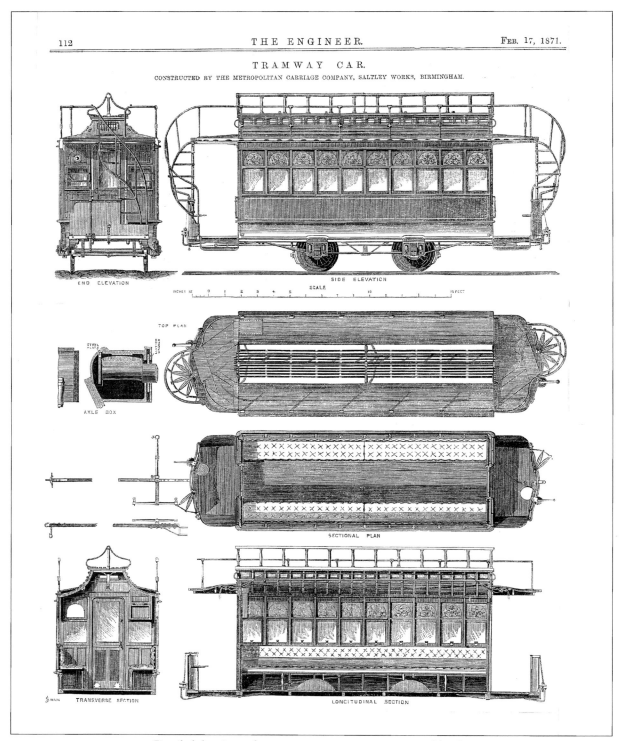

Detailed drawings of a contemporary tramcar constructed by the
Metropolitan Carriage Company of Birmingham for a London Company.
From *The Engineer* of 17 February 1871.

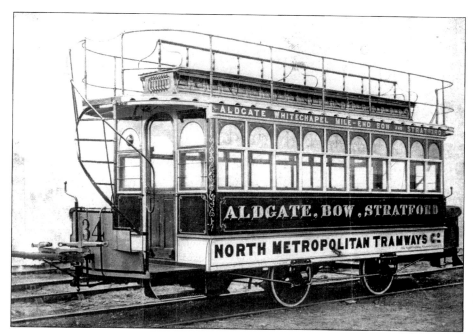

Left. Record photograph a knife-board seat car built c1870 by the Metropolitan Carriage Company for the North Metropolitan Tramway Co of London, similar to that in the previous illustration.

Below. One of the earliest Geneva horse cars photographed at the terminus of the initial line to Carouge. These first cares were constructed by Prentiss in Birkenhead, possibly contracted to him by the General Rolling Stock Company of London.

Pre-1866 Horse Tramways Outside USA

1853	21 November	Paris	Chemin de Fer Americain
1858	1 January	Mexico City	Ferro-carril de Tacubaya
1858	10 June	Santiago	Ferro-carril del Sur
1859	31 January	Rio de Janiero	Carris de Ferro da Cidade a Tijuca
1859	20 September	Havana	Ferro-carril Urbano de la Habana
1860	3 August	Birkenhead	Birkenhead Street Railway Co
1861	23 March	London	Marble Arch Street Railway Co.
1861	15 April	London	Westminster Street Railway Co.
1861	15 August	London	Surrey Side Street Railway Co.
1861	11 September	Toronto	Toronto Street Railway Co
1861	27 November	Montreal	Montreal City Passenger Railway Co
1861	23 December	Sydney	Pitt Street
1862	1 January	Darlington	Darlington Street Railway Co.
1862	13 January	Potteries	Staffordshire Potteries Street Rly Co
1862	19 June	Geneva	Tramway Genève – Carouge
1863	1 May	Cape Town	Cape Town & Green Point Tmy Co
1863	14 July	Buenos Aires	Aduana Nueva – Center
1863	8 September	St Petersburg	Znamenskaya Sq – Vasilyevsky Island
1863	22 October	Copenhagen	Copenhagen Railway Company
1864	25 June	The Hague	Dutch Tramway Company
1864	12 September	Geneva	Tramway Genève – Chêne
1865	22 June	Berlin	Berliner Pferde-Eisenbahn Ges
1865	4 October	Vienna	Schaeck-Jaquet & Cie

Dramatis Personae

G F Train brought into the arena of early street railway construction several individuals, some of whom played a significant role in the unfolding drama. They are listed alphabetically, not in order of the impact each had. This is considered a suitable way to summarise the contributions of each.

Bruce, George Barclay (1 October 1821–25 August 1908)
A renowned (later) civil engineer employed by Train as 'surveyor' for some of his early lines. He was named as joint engineer for the Staffordshire Potteries tramway, but most of his career was spent on main line railways, notably in India.

Bryan
In Train's autobiography 'Bryan' is named as manager of the Birkenhead Street Railway Company. No contemporary trace of any employee of this name has been found. Train may have intended Peniston (q.v.)

Burn, Charles
London based civil engineer who wrote *'On the Construction of Horse Railways for Branch Lines and for Street Traffic'*, published in April 1860, which Train might have been advised to study, as adherence to it might have avoided many of the subsequent pitfalls of Train's chosen designs. (Burn patented a design of grooved girder rail.) Train described Burn as a 'contractor' at Birkenhead, but Hathaway claimed to be the constructor of all six of Train's English lines. Burn claimed to have been the original engineer of the Amsterdam and North Sea Ship Canal, and was a director of many companies, including the Tavistock Iron Works and the Robertsfors Iron Works Co Ltd in Sweden. One director of the latter company was J O Tilston, also on the board of the General Rolling Stock Company Ltd.

Easton, Alexander (see also Part One) (c April 1828–??)
In his autobiography Train refers to 'Easton' as one of his contractors. This *could* be a reference to Alexander Easton, who – as it has been noted in the first section of this work – was involved in promotion and construction of early tramways in Canada and America. No contemporary reference has been found of involvement by Easton in England, all six of Train's tramways being constructed by Charles Hathaway, so perhaps Train's memory was playing him false – again. Alexander Easton was born in Dorset in 1828 and emigrated to America 21 years later. In his speech at the opening of the Toronto tramway, Easton still referred to himself as 'an Englishman''. He was author of the book published in Philadelphia in 1859 *'A Practical Treatise on Street or Horse-drawn Railways'*, which shows a comprehensive knowledge of affairs relative to existing lines.

Hall, Benjamin (8 November 1802–27 April 1867)
Son of an industrialist, who studied as a civil engineer prior to entering politics; initially (1831) as Whig MP for Monmouth, then in 1837 returned to represent Marylebone, London. He was responsible for an Act

which established the Metropolitan Board of Works, becoming its first Commissioner. He oversaw the erection of the Clock Tower of the Houses of Parliament, the main bell of which is named 'Big Ben' supposedly after him. Implacably opposed to street tramways, this is believed to have to have been the consequence of an accident to his carriage when crossing a waggonway in his Welsh constituency. He was largely responsible for the failure in March 1858 of the Bill for street tramways in London introduced by the London Omnibus Tramways Company (promoted following the successful Paris operation). Became Baron Llanover in 1859 and led vociferous opposition to Train's attempts to establish a tramway presence in London.

Hathaway, Charles (7 November 1824–2 July 1903)
Born in Grafton, Massachusetts, he traced his ancestry back to Lucy Hathaway, sister of Anne, wife of William

Photograph of Charles Hathaway with his obituary.

Shakespeare. He contracted to built several US railroads before, in 1857, turning to street railway construction in Philadelphia. Three years later with Train's active encouragement he joined him in England to act as contractor for all six English street railways, trading as Charles Hathaway & Co. At some date between 1861 and 1862, Hathaway and Prentiss joined forces in Birkenhead as 'builders of railroad cars', a short-lived partnership which was dissolved before the end of July 1862 when Hathaway returned to America. In an interview published in 1892 (then subsequently reiterated in his obituary) he claimed '... The cars for these roads were built in Philadelphia and shipped in sections to Birkenhead where they were put together, painted and fitted for service in car shops owned by [me] ...' This statement, which has been repeated down the years by more than one writer, does not (in this writer's opinion) reflect accurately the genesis of the first Birkenhead street railway vehicles. On his return to America in July 1862, he founded a construction company which became Hathaway & Robison, his partner being his son-in-law, who ran the business after Hathaway's retiral. This company constructed more than 130 street railways in the United States of America.

Johnson, Richard W
Proprietor of the Railway Carriage Company of Oldbury by Birmingham who received orders from Train for tramcars for both Birmingham and London. At least one (and possibly more) were completed, one being exhibited in London in October 1860. For some undetermined reason Train refused to accept them and a court case ensued. This dispute appears to have been resolved, the probable conclusion being that the two completed cars (and fittings for four more) were exported to Melbourne, for a tramway which was never constructed. Johnson's company later built a small number of tramway cars, and in 1886 was reconstituted as the Oldbury Railway Carriage & Wagon Co Ltd.

Laird, John (14 June 1805–29 October 1874)
John Laird was born in Greenock, but left while an infant when his parents moved to Liverpool and then

Birkenhead. He was fundamental in the establishment of Birkenhead as a major manufacturing town, his father having founded an Iron Works there. Laird established a ship building yard, using iron and boiler-making techniques for the hulls and by 1834 supplied the CSS *Alabama* to the state of Georgia. He played a fundamental role in the development of Birkenhead, becoming its first Mayor. He probably saw Train's tramway proposals as an exciting modern way to advance the Burgh. When Birkenhead was established as a Parliamentary Borough in 1861, Laird was elected as its first (Conservative) Member of Parliament. His shipyard was constructing two ram vessels for the Confederate States Navy when the UK government forcibly suspended work on them. The two vessels, which were to have been named *Mississippi* and *North Carolina* were then completed and taken into the British Royal Navy as HMS *Wivern* and HMS *Scorpion* respectively.

Main, Robert Hall (1816(?) − 4 April 1887)

Main was established as a successful coach-builder in Birkenhead before Train appeared on the scene. A Scot, born in Stirling, it is likely that he was apprenticed to the renowned coach building business established there in 1802 by Messrs Croall & Kinross. His aunt (Janet Main) married George Kinross in 1809. Main's first workshop may have been in Gill Street Liverpool where a fire in Mr **D** [sic] Main's coachworks was reported at the beginning of December 1856[215]. However by September 1858 Main was based in Birkenhead, where he built the Curtis Patent road-rail omnibus (the '*Enterprise*') used on the Liverpool's 'Line of Docks' railway[216]. Main designed and patented road/rail wheels (number 1046 of 26 April 1859) but these were not fitted to this vehicle. Train's autographical statement 'Thanks to my early Methodist training; I have never knowingly told a lie' must surely indicate that his [Train's] assertion in 1860 that it was Main who built the first four cars for the Birkenhead street railway be given full and proper credibility. Main is also given acknowledgement for these vehicles in every reference in the contemporary press. It was also recorded of the two cars supplied for the street railway in Sydney that 'The carriages are labelled Robert Main, Coach Builder, Birkenhead, George Francis Train's Patent''. Two further cars were built by Main, to the instruction of Thomas Evans, to run in opposition on the Birkenhead street railway − 'similar to those already running''. So far as is known, these eight (or nine if the Curtis vehicle is included) are the only tramway cars known to have been built by Main. At the beginning of 1860, his workshop was in the yard of the Woodside Hotel, but during March of that year this was advertised for let.[217] He then moved across the street and relocated to 26 Canning Street, premises formerly used as the Holly Bank Academy.[218] It was here that Main built the first tramway cars *used* in the United Kingdom and where the celebratory meal at the inauguration was held.

Musgrove, Ralph Noel

Manager of Birkenhead Street Railway Company 1 December 1860 − October 1861. Had been a steamship's purser, but was sent by Train to New York Philadelphia to learn to manage a street railway. He returned from America in November 1860 and was employed at a salary of 5% of gross profit. When dismissed, took the company to court for loss of earnings. (Gave a lecture on his travels in Peru, so must have been well qualified to oversee England's first tramway!) Last recorded as licensee of a restaurant in Lower Castle Street, Liverpool

Palles, Andrew Christopher (1830−?)

Civil Engineer in Philadelphia who apparently was engaged by the American & European Tramway Company to supervise construction of the Birkenhead line. Frequently credited with design of first cars for Birkenhead. Went to act as engineer on street railway proposals for Dublin, and may thereafter have settled in Ireland.

Peniston, Richard (later 'Penniston')

Secretary of Birkenhead Street Railway Co from August 1860 to June 1861, possibly formerly a shipping agent. No further details uncovered.

Prentiss, Elijah Freeman (25 July 1822–?)
Prentiss was a Philadelphia manufacturing chemist, with several patents to his credit. He wrote to Train in December 1860, giving details of street railways in the city '... if so many railroads can succeed with us, what, in all probability, would be the result of one or two main lines, with branches, either in London or other cities? ... Great improvements have been introduced since the first roads were built, and Europe can now avail itself of America's experiments. Depend upon it, there is nothing that will prove so acceptable to the European public as a complete system of horse railways.'[219] By the end of March 1861 he had joined Train in England[220] and was employed as manager of Birkenhead Street Railway Company, then as Managing Director by December of the same year. He entered into a short-lived partnership with Charles Hathaway as constructors of railroad cars, and on dissolution of that arrangement, in July 1862, probably took on George Starbuck junior in his place. Cars credited as constructed by Prentiss & Co were for Darlington (2), Staffordshire Potteries (2), Geneva (6?), and Copenhagen (probably the first two deliveries of 6 and 5 cars respectively). These latter vehicles may in fact have been built to the order of the United Kingdom Rolling Stock Company, set up to provide and lease rolling stock for newly established (impecunious) companies. The partnership with Starbuck was dissolved in May 1865, Prentiss by then having returned to the United States.

Samuel, James, CE (1824 – 25 May 1874)
Consulting civil engineer who advised on several railway and tramway proposals, including, from 1846, the Eastern Counties Railway. He acted for the French consortium which attempted to obtain comprehensive powers for passenger tramways in London in 1857. This, the London Omnibus Tramway Co Ltd, proposed eight miles of route, applied for by way of a House of Commons Bill which failed at its second reading. After 1860 Samuel advised Train, although the original [Omnibus] company then unsuccessfully attempted to re-invent itself in opposition to Train. It is recorded of

Samuel that '... his taste for inventing amounted to a passion ...' Perhaps, had he advised Train against the use of the step rail, the eventual outcome may have been completely different.

Sheldon, William H (8 December 1811 – 8 December 1883)
Involved in operation and development of stage coaches in the north west of England, he was one of the founders of the General Omnibus Company, operating horse buses in the capital. In 1861, when Train commenced operations in London, Sheldon joined him, providing horses for the various lines. His brother John was, for a time, manager of the Surrey Side Street Railway. He then, in association with his son, was involved in construction and operation of tramways in Geneva (1862), Copenhagen (1863), Brussels (1869), Madrid (1871) Bucharest (1874) and Bremen (1876); these may have resulted from his involvement with the British & Foreign Tramways Company who had also promoted the tramways of Bucharest, Neuilly (Paris), Glasgow, Bristol and Aberdeen and who set up a tramcar construction business, the Tramway Car & Works Company of Greenwich and Glasgow. Sheldon was a director of the Metropolitan Tramway Company by 1870. Sheldon's obituary prompted an immediate response from Charles Burn CE 'The concession for the Geneva tramways was obtained by me and they were built and worked by me in co-partnership with the late Edward Sharpe MA, Mr Sheldon having been our salaried manager for the working only'. Sheldon's death notice had him as dying on his 72nd birthday; obituaries credited him as then being eighty years of age – an object lesson in not believing all you read.

Shelley, Sir John, 7th Baronet (18 March 1808 – 28 January 1867)
Tory politician first elected 1830–32, later MP for Westminster 1852–65. Was vehemently opposed to the principle of street railways or tramways – even before the unfortunate case brought against him by Train's landlord as detailed above. Subsequently appears to have taken every possible opportunity (either personally or

by proxy) as a member of the Metropolitan Board of Works to ensure that the London street railways were as short-lived as possible. Died before the eventual universal acceptance of tramways as an efficient means of mass public transport.

Starbuck, George junior (5 January 1834 – 14 May 1917) Born in Nantucket from a family which had settled in America by 1635. A George M Starbuck is listed in an 1855 Boston directory as a carriage builder, this possibly being George (*senior*) – and most likely the father of 'our' George. In business as a commission merchant in Melbourne in 1854, he there met George Francis Train and entered into a partnership with him and Joshua Crane on 1 November 1855. When Train left Australia in 1855 so that his wife would have their first child on American soil, Starbuck was left in control of his Australian affairs. The partnership was dissolved on 31 October 1857, the business declared insolvent a year

later. Starbuck travelled to England in 1860 where (he said) he invested £2000 capital into Train's street railway business. Starbuck acted as manager or secretary of the three street railways in London and became liquidator of the Surrey Side line. In 1862, when Train returned to the USA, he joined – as junior partner – with E F Prentiss (on borrowed capital of £1500) as petroleum distillers and builders of street railway carriages. [Petroleum was then also known as 'American Earth Oil'] At this time the partnership supplied (possibly to the order of the General Rolling Stock Company *or* the United Kingdom Railway Rolling Stock Company) tramway vehicles to Geneva (1862) Buenos Aires (probably) and Copenhagen (both 1863). These initial cars followed closely the design and layout of the cars imported into England from Philadelphia builders. This partnership was dissolved in May 1865 and exactly one year later Starbuck was declared bankrupt, debtors receiving 5/- in the £. Starbuck somehow managed to continue on

Several record photographs of Starbuck's products have survived, including this of an example for the London Tramway Company of the early 1870s.

Interior of a London tram supplied by Starbuck. This is a double deck car,
the iron ladder can be seen through the end windows. From the *Graphic*.

his own account, using the same premises at the Great Float, Birkenhead, until he was yet again declared bankrupt, with his stock-in-trade (including two tramcar bodies) auctioned off in June 1867. He re-commenced once more on his own account, now trading as George Starbuck & Co, from workshops at a new location in Cleveland Street Birkenhead, this incorporated as a limited company on 12 September 1871. [His recollection of dates supplied to his various bankruptcy hearings is remarkably imprecise.] A new company, Starbuck Carriage and Wagon Co Ltd was registered on 6 November 1872, until it, too, went into liquidation in 1886, the effects auctioned in the middle of October. The company in its various guises constructed a large number of tramway cars, with a considerable percentage for overseas customers. An 1868 example

(Brussels no. 7) is to be found in the tram museum at Woluwe, also two examples of the firm's work which were exported to Oporto in 1874 still exist, one (no. 8) at their Massarelos tram museum, another (no. 9) at the National Tramway Museum at Crich in Derbyshire.

Train, George Francis (24 March 1829 – 5 January 1904) Train's life was so full that an autobiography and more than one biographies exist. The former was dictated entirely from memory in July and August 1902, when he was in his 74th year, and must be read with this in mind. Several of his statements therein do not accord with the contemporary record, where this has been examined.

There is no intention here to relate detail of Train's many and varied exploits – for that detail any interested

Above. No photograph of George Starbuck Junior has been located, but after some searching his grave, and that of his wife, was located in Flaybridge cemetery, Birkenhead. (Robert Jones)

Right. There is no shortage of photographs of 'Citizen' Train. He was a self-publicist of note, and handed out carte-de-visite photographs of himself given any opportunity. This one dates to c1875.

party should refer to the works mentioned. He made his first circumnavigation of the globe in 1870, said to be the inspiration for Jules Verne's *Around the World in Eighty Days*. Train ran for President of the USA in 1872 and went down in history as the only presidential candidate – ever – to charge admission to his election rallies. Train was described as a cross between Mark Twain and B T Barnum – and also as 'a most bumptious specimen of his bumptious kind ...' But even Mark Twain had a highly jaundiced opinion of Train '... was there ever such a world of egotism stuffed into one carcass before ... our blowing, shrieking, ranting lightning express has degenerated into a poor, homely, inconsequential baggage-Train after all". In his later years Train lived alone in a single small hotel room – he called himself the 'Great American Crank' – perhaps

with good reason, and spent much time chatting with children in Madison Square Park. He died of a heart attack, with thousands of people lining the streets to pay their last respects, including it is said, 2000 children.

Trimston, R
Named as secretary of the Birkenhead Street Railway Company at the opening of that line in August 1860; probably a misprint for *Peniston* (q.v.)

Wiswell, Thomas M
An American Civil Engineer who apparently was brought in to supervise reconstruction of the Birkenhead line in 1863. He subsequently acted as manager of that Street Railway Co. from November 1863 until after 1867.

Top. In his years of opulence, Train and his family owned this large villa 'Showandsee' on Bellevue Avenue, Newport, Rhode Island. It was damaged in a fire in the 1970s. (Newport Historical Society, Rhode Island)

Above. Engraving from *'Frank Leslie's Illustrated Newspaper'* dated 25 May 1889 and captioned there 'New York: George Francis Train gives his young friends a May-day party in Central Park'.

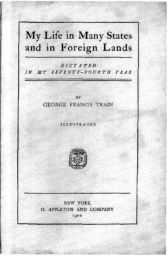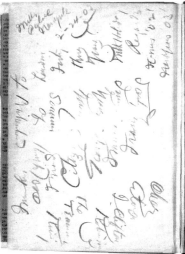

Top. G F Train entertaining more friends at the Mills Hotel New York, where he lived out the last seven years of his life in a single bedroom. The dining room presents a rather Spartan appearance, but provides a remarkable record, a contrast from that of 1860s London.

Above. In 1903 Train sent a copy of his autobiography to James Clifton Robinson, inscribed in his inimitable fashion. Dated 25 February, it is now in a private collection. The comments in Train's typical blunt blue crayon are not easy to decipher; he died less than a year later.

THE GENERAL ROLLING STOCK COMPANY Limited.

(Capital £150,000, in 15,000 Shares of £10 each.
With power to increase.)

Deposit 10s. per Share on application, and 30s. on allotment, and the remainder in Calls not exceeding £2 10s. per Share, at intervals of not less than three months.

DIRECTORS.

George Brockelbank, Esq., Greenwich.
John Pope Hennessy, Esq., M.P., Director of the Wellington and Cheshire Junction Railway.
James Morrish, Esq., Director of the Hereford, Hay, and Brecon Railway.
Sir Edwin Pearson, F.R.S., Director of the Scottish Australian Investment Company.
Richard Kyrke Penson, Esq., Director of the Aberystwith and Welsh Coast Railway.
W. Edgcumbe Rendle, Esq., Director of the South Devon and Tavistock Railway.
Alfred Terry, Esq., Colliery Proprietor, Swansea.
Joseph Tilston, Esq., Director of the Amman (Aberdare) Colliery Company.

With power to add to their number.)

AUDITORS.

Messrs. Coleman, Turquand, Youngs, and Co., 16, Tokenhouse-yard.
John Gordon, Esq., 9, Mincing-lane.

SOLICITORS.

Messrs. Davidson, Bradbury, Hardwick, and Carr, Weavers' Hall, 22, Basinghall-street.

BANKERS.

London—The Metropolitan and Provincial Bank, 75, Cornhill, E.C.
Liverpool—The Alliance Bank of London and Liverpool, 22, the Albany.
Birmingham—Messrs. Moilliett and Son.

BROKERS.

London—Messrs. J. and J. Whitehead, 8, Moorgate-street.
Liverpool—Messrs. G. and T. Irvine, 7, India-buildings.
Birmingham—J. W. Hamilton, Esq., 20, Ann-street.
SECRETARY, pro. tem.—Mr. E. Murphy.
TEMPORARY OFFICES.—15, Tokenhouse-yard, E.C.

This Company is established for the purpose of purchasing, maintaining, and leasing carriages and waggons to railway companies, collieries, and commercial firms, in the United Kingdom and elsewhere. Local companies of this description have been formed from time to time, as the demand for increased carrying accommodation has been developed, but the existence of these companies has been almost unknown beyond the immediate districts in which they have been originated, while at the same time such companies are amongst the most successful undertakings of the day, distributing large dividends to the shareholders and accumulating ample reserve funds, as will be seen from the following statements:—

Name of Company.	Amount of Share.	Dividend per Cent.	Reserve.	Price.
	£		£	Premium.
Midland Waggon Co.	50	10*	58,910	100 to 105 per ct.
The Railway Rolling Stock Association	10	9	20,504	35 to 40 "
Birmingham Waggon Co.	10	10	10,308	40 to 45 "
Gloucester Waggon Co.	10	10	3,500	35 to 40 "

And occasionally large bonuses.

It is also proposed to take special powers to lease complete lines of railway, and to work them at a fixed rate equal to a certain agreed per centage on capital. Although this portion of the business has been carried on with great success by private capitalists, it has not as yet been undertaken by any of the existing companies; but the Directors of the General Rolling Stock Company (Limited are satisfied, from their practical knowledge, that a very large and profitable trade may be derived from the establishment of this branch of the Company's operations, as the whole of the stock will thus be kept in constant work. The Directors have, moreover, the prospect of entering upon a contract of this description immediately they are prepared to undertake it; but no such contract will be taken without the sanction of the shareholders in general meeting.

The want of the accommodation about to be afforded by this Company has long been acknowledged; and it is manifest, that if the demand of the several provincial districts is equal to the profitable employment of a very large amount of capital, the operations of a Company with an enlarged sphere of action, promise still more satisfactory results.

It is not proposed at present to expend any capital in the establishment of works or plant for building purposes, but to obtain the Company's stock, from time to time, upon the most advantageous terms; thus the capital of the Company will at all times be represented by an absolute and available security.

The shareholders will incur no liability beyond the amount of shares allotted to them.

Applications for shares must be made in the form annexed to the prospectus. Each applicant will be required to pay into the bankers of the Company 10s. per share on the number of shares applied for, and, upon allotment, to make a further payment of 30s. per share on the shares allotted to him.

If no allotment be made, the deposit will be returned without deduction; but the directors reserve the power to commence business as soon as a sufficient number of shares are subscribed for the purpose.

Prospectuses and forms of application for shares may be had of the Brokers, Messrs. J. and J. Whitehead, 8, Moorgate-street; the Solicitors, Messrs. Davidson, Bradbury, Hardwick, and Carr, 22, Basinghall-street; and at the temporary offices, 15, Tokenhouse-yard.

THE ROLLING STOCK COMPANY of IRELAND (Limited).

For the Building, Sale, and Letting on Lease, or otherwise, of Railway Carriages and Waggons.

Capital £200,000, in 20,000 Shares of £10 each. Deposit on application £1 per share, and on allotment £1. Calls not to exceed £1 per share, and three months' interval between two successive calls.

DIRECTORS.

George Breginton, Esq., Torrington, Devon, Director of the North Devon Railway.
George Chambers, Esq., 11, George-yard, Lombard-street, Vice-Chairman of the Cork and Youghal Railway.
J. W. Cusack, Esq., 13, Lancaster-gate, Hyde-park.
D. J. Henry, Esq., 1, Camden-square, Chairman of the Tewkesbury and Malvern Railway.
Major the Hon. G. F. Jocelyn, Chairman of the Dundalk Steam Packet Company.
Jasper Wilson Johns, Esq., Great Cumberland-street, Hyde-park, Director of the Oswestry and Newtown Railway, and the Mid Wales Railway.
J. Digges Latouche, Esq., Dublin, Director of the Midland Great Western Railway.
David M'Birney, Esq., Director of the Enniskillen and Bundoran Railway.
C. H. Maude, Esq., 19, St George's-square, Belgravia.
Valentine O'Brien O'Connor, Esq., Chairman of the Cork and Bandon Railway, and Director of the Great Southern and Western Railway.
W. F. Drought Stephens, Esq., Cleveland-gardens, Hyde-park.
James Stirling, Esq., Dublin, Director of the Midland Great Western of Ireland Railway, and the Dublin and Wicklow Railway.

BANKERS.

London—Metropolitan and Provincial Bank, Cornhill.
Dublin—Provincial Bank of Ireland and its Branches.

BROKERS.

London.—Messrs. Staples and Schlotel, 2, Spread Eagle-court, Royal Exchange.
Dublin.—Messrs. Boyle, Low, Pim, and Co., College-green; and Edward Fox, Esq., 51, Dame-street.

AUDITORS.

London.—Messrs. Quilter, Ball, Jay, and Co., 3, Moorgate-street.
Dublin.—Richard Martin, Esq. (Messrs. John Martin and Son;
W. T. Stephens, Esq. (Messrs. Courtney and Stephens).

SOLICITORS.

London.—Messrs. Kimberley and Pope, 26, Old Broad-st., City.
Dublin.—James Malley, Esq., 48, Upper Sackville-street.
SECRETARY—Eugene Hay, Esq.
TEMPORARY OFFICES—London: 26, Old Broad-street.

PROSPECTUS.

English enterprise has of late years opened up no channel for financial investment at once so safe, legitimate, and profitable as rolling stock companies, or, as they are more commonly termed, waggon companies. The best indication of this, and of the opinion still entertained by capitalists of schemes of this character, is shown by the fact that the shares of all the leading companies are at premiums ranging from 35 to 100 per cent., and that the minimum dividend, after setting aside very large reserve funds, has never sunk below 9 per cent. The Gloucester Waggon Company, which is the most recent, has paid 10 per cent. dividend in its first year. Its £10 shares are now worth nearly £14, and it has a reserve fund of nearly £4,000. (See annexed table.)

It is, however, remarkable that, while uniform success has been obtained in the face of vigorous competition, and in supplying mainly the wants of English railways, the sister country has been wholly unprovided for, and this field the present company now proposes in the first instance to occupy.

An important feature in this undertaking, and which may be almost set down as a guarantee for its success, is the fact that the Irish gauge is different from either of the English gauges, and consequently the rolling stock manufactured in England for Ireland cannot be run over the English lines to the port of embarkation, but has to be put on trucks and transported across the Channel at a very heavy cost for freight and charges, amounting on an average to about seven and a half per cent. on the selling price.

English Companies are not usually their own builders, the contracts being generally undertaken by private firms. This Company will reserve the option to construct and maintain its own stock, and the advantage consequently accruing to the Company in the way of first profits must necessarily be considerable.

The operations of the Company will be commenced in Dublin, where the directors have the offer of several suitable sites on advantageous terms, and where many of the existing railway companies are prepared to avail themselves of the facilities which this Company will place at their disposal.

The Company will be prepared to undertake the supply of the entire rolling stock for railways, or to lease the working of lines, finding locomotive power, carriages and waggons, or to contract for their maintenance and repair.

The Directors feel that it is unnecessary to direct specific attention to the steady and progressive character of railway enterprise in Ireland, or to the remunerative character of all the arterial lines as a medium for the profitable investment of capital.

Prospectuses and forms of application may be obtained of the brokers, or of the solicitors, or at the temporary offices of the Company.

The deposit of £1 upon each share applied for must be paid to the Company's bankers previously to the application being sent in. This sum will be returned in full if no allotment is made to the applicant.

The following table, compiled from authentic sources, shows the present prosperous condition of rolling stock companies in England:—

Name of Company.	Amount of Share.	Dividend per Cent.	Reserve.	Price.
	£		£	Premium.
Midland Waggon Co.	50	10*	58,910	100 to 105 per ct.
The Railway Rolling Stock Association	10	9	20,504	35 to 40 "
Birmingham Waggon Co.	10	10	10,308	40 to 45 "
Gloucester Waggon Co.†	10	10‡	3,500	35 to 40 "

* And occasionally large bonuses.
† This Company build and maintain their own stock.
‡ In the first year's working.

APPLICATION FOR SHARES.

To the Directors of the Rolling Stock Company of Ireland (Limited).

Gentlemen,—Having paid £ to your bankers, I request you will allot to me shares in the Rolling Stock Company of Ireland (Limited), or any less number, which I hereby agree to accept, and to pay the further sum of £1 per share on the number allotted to me, and all future calls when required; and I further authorise and empower you to insert my name in the register of shareholders of the Company for the number of shares that may be allotted to me.

Name in full...........................
Profession or description...........................
Date........................... 1862.
Residence in full...........................
Signature...........................

Adjacent adverts inviting subscriptions to the General Rolling Stock Coy and the Rolling Stock Coy of Ireland.

Appendix

The General Rolling Stock Company (Limited)

This company was floated in mid July 1862 with as its object the provision or supply (but not actual construction) of rolling stock for lease to minor railways and tramways which would consequently be spared this expense in their formative years. The initial capital was £150,000 in shares of £10 each and the directors included senior officers from several small railways, plus John Pope Hennessey, a highly respected Member of Parliament who later became one of Britain's premier diplomats. The first (temporary) company secretary was an E Murphy, operating from 15 Tokenhouse Yard. Floated at precisely the same time was another – nominally – separate company, the Rolling Stock Company of Ireland (Ltd) with twelve (mostly Irish) different directors and Eugene Hay as temporary company secretary at 26 Old Broad Street. This had capital of £200,000 in £10 shares. At the end of August the first company advertised for a permanent secretary, and by the beginning of December this post was occupied by J Howard Russel, who operated from 92 Cannon Street London EC, the two companies now referred to as 'united'. The Irish company (according to its prospectus) *did* intend to manufacture railway rolling stock, quoting the problems caused by the lack of such facility in Ireland, and the difficulties thus induced by construction in England of rolling stock to the Irish 5 ft 3 ins gauge, which would be overcome. It was stated that all existing such stock in Ireland to that date had been built in England.[221]

It would appear that both companies were created by one mind, but the entire establishment of each was completely different from the other – except for one of the banks involved, (the Metropolitan and Provincial) which served both. The fact that the two companies were very soon 'united' would suggest that this had been the plan from the start. It is also possible to surmise that the rapid failure of the united undertaking came not entirely a surprise to some of those involved. It is also noteworthy that the bank which laid out most, and which lost most, was not the Metropolitan and Provincial, but the Alliance, which appears to have had no involvement in the Irish venture.

By the end of 1862 the company was declaring that it had for hire a large number of goods wagons and had works in London and Dublin. The former was located at the 'Railway Works, Goswell Street'; the latter at the Seville Works in Dublin[222]. Early the following year a statement advised that it had taken over the established London contractor, coal merchant and railway carriage builder, Charles Cave Williams, this apparently despite the declaration in the prospectus that it would not indulge in the business of manufacture! Cave Williams had constructed much railway rolling stock at his establishment in Glasshouse Yard, Goswell Street, including coaches for the Oxford, Worcester and Wolverhampton Railway Company (allegedly known as the Old Worse and Worse) a line absorbed into the Great Western Railway in 1863. The Seville Iron Works

Left. Rather indistinct view, but probably recording the opening procession of horse trams in Buenos Aires on 14 July 1863. The 'Birkenhead' style of the double deck vehicles is apparent; current opinion is that these first cars were shipped out from England, where the owning company was founded. (Allen Morrison Collection)

Below. One of Copenhagen's Birkenhead style cars, in 1865, at the western Frederiksberg Runddel terminus. Another purchase probably arranged through the General Rolling Stock Company.

in Dublin was a long established business then owned by a Scotsman, William Robinson, who apparently saw this as an opportunity to diversify. This company had made castings for I K Brunel's Wye River railway bridge at Chepstow in 1852, but in April 1863 advised that it was giving up manufacture of iron bedsteads, as the premises had been sold to the Rolling Stock Company of Ireland.[223] This may appear to have been premature, as the Works remained in operation for several years subsequently.

Another coachbuilder and rolling stock manufacturer caught up in the tangled affairs of these companies was Shackleford, Ford & Company of Cheltenham and Swansea. In August 1862 Mr Shackleford, the principal partner, purchased shares of the General Rolling Stock Company of Ireland, paying the initial £2000 due on application, but on the understanding that he would subsequently receive rolling stock orders, to be paid for by the later calls on these shares. However, when the directors of the two Rolling Stock companies announced their amalgamation intention he asked for return of his cash – and received it – but was then taken to court (unsuccessfully) by the liquidator for his contribution due on further calls.[224] The company had contracts to construct wagons and vans for the Great Western Railway, but was reconstructed as a limited liability company in May 1866, the Cheltenham & Swansea Wagon Company Limited.

It also appears probable (but not confirmed) that tramway rolling stock for lines at Buenos Aires, St Petersburg and Copenhagen (all opened in 1863) was built in England, but supplied through the General Rolling Stock Company (or the United Kingdom Railway Rolling Stock Company). An ambitious dividend of 10% was paid to shareholders following the first four months of operation.

The first vehicles for the Dutch Tramways Company were obtained through the General Rolling Stock Company, and probably constructed by Charles Cave Williams of London.

This view of double deck (or 'imperial') car 4 of the initial batch was taken soon after the opening on 25 June 1864 and was recorded by the Oude Kirk in Scheveningen.

The cars for the Dutch Tramway Company were also probably ordered through the General Rolling Stock Company. This view shows car number 1 at the Badhuis in Scheveningen shortly after the opening. This single-deck car was for first-class only. On the rear platform the conductor has his trumpet at the ready to signal departure; it was a requirement that candidates for this post had to be accomplished in the instrument. (Jan H Vis Collection)

An early horse tramway opened in the Cape of Good Hope between Cape Town and Green Point on 1 May 1863, using two cars reported to have been constructed locally by a Mr Harris and named *Victoria* and *Albert*.[225] A photograph of the first car shows some similarity to those to be supplied for the first tramway in Holland, and despite the confident assertion of the local press, it has also been stated that 'there were no engineering works in Cape Town at that time which could have turned out such a complicated item from basic materials'.[226] However the 1863 photograph bears an imprint of 'Davis & Soper, Shippers'. This partnership was formed in 1860, then between 1863 and 1870 operated from 14 Fenchurch Street London, hence the balance of probability would tend to suggest that the two initial cars were, indeed, shipped from London, and

could have been supplied by the General Rolling Stock Company, *possibly* products of the carriage works of Charles Cave Williams (see page 142).

According to a work published in the Netherlands, the General Rolling Stock Company supplied vehicles to the Dutch Tramway Company Limited.[227] Initially known as the Holland Tramway Company this was floated in London in March 1864 with, as secretary, G F Smith based at 16 Cannon Street.[228] The chairman was John Chynoweth of Holland Park. Initial capital was £50,000 and an announcement was made immediately that a contract worth £40,000 had been entered into with a responsible English contracting company to purchase land, make lines, provide rolling stock and horses – and have the line up and running by May coming.

'Imperial', or double-deck, horse car of the Dutch Tramway Company. Car 7, apparently photographed at the same location and time as that opposite. Access to the top deck seating was by way of vertical ladders, which can be seen behind the driver. (Jan H Vis Collection)

A concession for a horse tramway (based on that operating in Paris) had been granted on 29 April 1862 to a Dutch engineer, Cornelis Soetens. This was to link the Hague with its coastal resort of Scheveningen but was withdrawn when he was unable to raise the necessary capital locally. On 15 August 1863 this license was made over to Neville Davidson Goldsmid, an Englishman who held a concession for gas supply in the Hague. Creation of the Dutch Tramway Company followed promptly, with the capital apparently raised without difficulty. Bankers to the Company were the Alliance Bank (again) who appear to have been heavily involved in several such speculative ventures of the General Rolling Stock Co type. A sub-contract for track laying is ascribed to Messrs Street and Marmont who commenced work in February 1864. The line ran from the Hotel Paulez on Korte Voorhaut in the centre of the Dutch seat of government as far as the Badhuis (Bathhouse) near the sea front in Scheveningen, described then as 'the Brighton of Holland' – a distance of just over three miles.[229] The outward line was by Koninginnegracht, along Badhausplien in Scheveningen returning by Keizerstraat and Oude Scheveningenweg to Kneuterdijk.

The company operated from its public opening on 23 June 1864 with a degree of difficulty, suffering badly from broken axles and wheels. The concession required that a regular service be provided, but this was achieved only with difficulty and the likely substitution on occasion of horse buses, of which the company owned two. Forty 'young and useful riding and driving horses' from the line were offered for sale in Colchester in Decem-

Inauguration of the first tramway in Cape Town, in the then British Cape Colony, on 1 May 1863. The initial cars may have been constructed in England, possibly supplied by the General Rolling Stock Company. The vertical ladder access to the top deck is reminiscent of the cars supplied to Sydney etc. (Courtesy South African Library, Cape Town)

ber 1865.[230] Then during the following year the complete enterprise, including the concession, the track, rolling and live stock was offered up to be sold by tender.[231] The asking price for the undertaking was then just £6,000. On January 27 1866 it was resolved to voluntarily wind up the company.[232]

This entire £40,000 contract had been taken on by Messrs Rose and Rouse, contractors, of 'the Strand in the County of Middlesex', who would almost certainly then sub-contract much of the work – probably including provision of the necessary rolling stock. Having apparently completed satisfactorily their part of the bargain, they were then required to take, in lieu of payment, £23,000 in shares of the company (very soon to be virtually worthless). Another bankruptcy later blamed on the collapse of the Dutch Tramway Company was that of William Pulsford France, of Paddington described as 'timber merchant, contractor

and manufacturer of railway keys'. He was due £9000 by Rose & Rouse, but probably saw little of it.[233]

Seven cars were eventually supplied for the line (probably built by Cave Williams), two single deck available at the opening, two double deck ('imperial') being added the following month. One of each type followed in August, with a final double deck in September. The three single-deck first class (1, 2, and 5) and four double-deck (3, 4, 6 and 7) were said to have been built entirely of mahogany. This would seem unlikely, but the appearance – if photographs are an accurate indication – is of vehicles devoid of a painted livery, apparently finished in varnished natural wood, the visible external panels indeed probably being of mahogany. The four 'imperial' cars were later used by the successor company, the Haagsche Tramway Maatschappij, which took over operation from 22 February 1867. Cave Williams exhibited a railway carriage at the London 1851 Great Exhibition, described as 'entirely built of East India teak, unpainted, as varnish only is used, allowing a damaged vehicle to be repaired and back at work in days ...'[234]

The Rolling Stock Company also involved itself with railway promotion, including major investment in a 15 mile long line from Barcelona to Granollers in Spain. However this entire house of cards fell apart on 27 January 1865 when a petition for winding-up was presented, resulting simultaneously in the failure of Cave Williams.[235] In February 1865 an order was put down for the winding up of the General Rolling Stock Company and when in March a liquidator (Mr Chatteris) was appointed details of the scandalous and highly speculative operations were exposed. The company never had more than £10,531 of working capital, but had borrowed £178,000 from the Alliance Bank. Liabilities amounted to £800,000, with Cave Williams due £15,000 for rolling stock built for the Granollers Railway. Listed under expenditure was a 'douceur' [sweetener] of £50,000 paid to the chairman – a local politician – of the Spanish railway (to ensure that the company was awarded the appropriate contracts) – plus a further sum of like amount for railway infrastructure. £50,000 in 1864 is equivalent at time of writing to over £30 million related to average earnings, much more if related to costs. Cave Williams owned 5000 fully paid shares in the General Rolling Stock Company (nominally worth £50,000) and £150,000 of the Granollers Railway stock.[236]

The failure of the General Rolling Stock Company was subsequently used to illustrate the scandal of investment in such highly speculative companies, this being held to be a prime example. Lawyers did very well from the ensuing resolution of the convoluted affairs of the company, which were not finally determined until mid 1874. Debtors were lucky to get 2d in the £, and the repercussions for the Alliance Bank were considerable[237].

Perhaps the oldest surviving tramcar in Europe is this example of the output from the works of George Starbuck.

Brussels number 7 was supplied in 1868 and can be seen at the Musee des Transports, Woluwe, Brussels.

The United Kingdom Railway Rolling Stock Co (Ltd)

This company, with objects almost replicating those of the General Rolling Stock Company, issued its prospectus in December 1862. With capital of £100,000 in shares of £10 each, its Chairman was John Biddulph, Chairman of the Llanelly Railway and Dock company, while another director was J T Pritchell, also on the board of the Copenhagen Railway Company. Secretary was William Cash of 13 Token-house Yard, London. [Is it a total coincidence that this address in adjacent to the office used by the company referred to above?] Much of the capital subscribed came from the Sheffield area. Pritchell may have been involved with supply of tram cars to Copenhagen through his connections in both countries. The company traded successfully for several years, returning dividends never less than 7% after the first year of trading. Unfortunately several contracts in the late 1860s were not honoured and the company was in liquidation by the end of 1871. Copenhagen is the only *known* potential tramway association.

Left. Advertisement for potential investors in the United Kingdom Railway Rolling Stock Company, which, surprisingly, appears only in a Birmingham newspaper of 12 December 1862.

Opposite. Generally fares on Train's lines were set at 2d per single journey, but advance purchase of eight tokens for 1s reduced this to 1½d. These were not, as has been suggested, issued as souvenirs. Tokens for use on Train's lines all appear to have had the same design on the reverse. In recent years modern 'facsimiles' have appeared for lines which never existed in reality.

Illustrated opposite are:
1. Standard design of reverse.
2. Reverse of 'facsimile' token, cruder detail and wheels below rail level.
3. Birkenhead obverse.
4, 5. Obverse and reverse of a white-metal token for Thomas Evans' short-lived bus and tram operation in Birkenhead.
6. Marble Arch obverse.
7. Westminster obverse.
8. Surrey Side obverse.
9. Darlington obverse.
10. Staffordshire Potteries obverse.
11. Obverse of modern production for non-existent Leicestershire Company.
12. Obverse of probable modern production for Warwickshire Company. [There is, however, always the possibility that Train ordered these in anticipation of this line being approved – he did, after all, order cars for this line!] (© London Transport Museum: 1,6,7,8. © National Tramway Museum: 3, 9.)

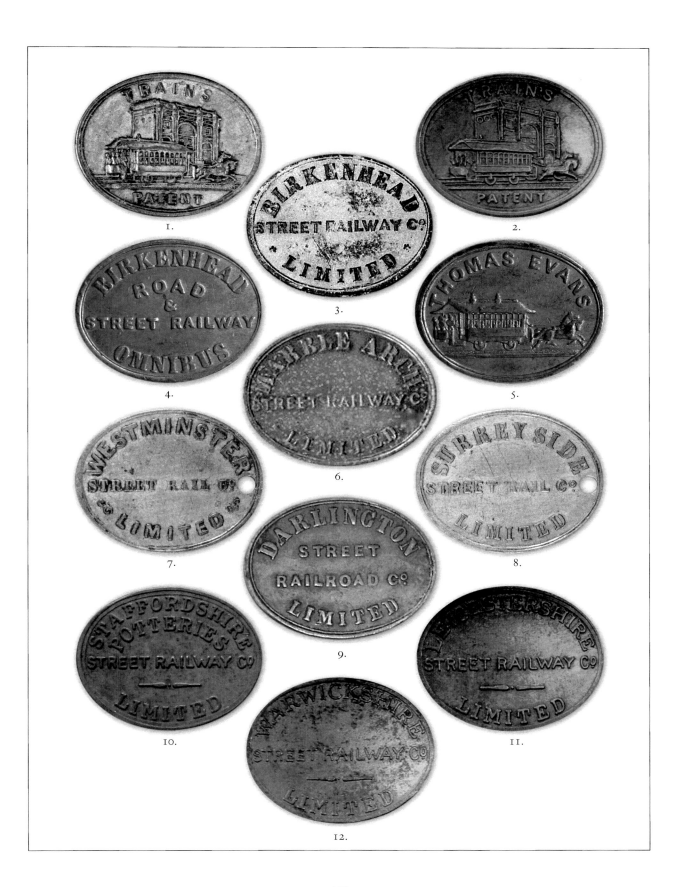

1.

2.

3.

4.

5.

6.

7.

8.

9.

10.

11.

12.

Notes

1 Train, GF *My Life in Many States and in Foreign Lands*, 1902

2 Robert, Jean *Les Tramways Parisiens*, 2nd Edition, 1959

3 Clark, D Kinnear *Tramways, Their Construction and Working*, 2nd Edition 1894

4 *The Engineer*, 23 April 1869

5 Grantham, John *Grantham's Steam car for Tramways*, 1874

6 Lee, C E *Journal of Transport History*, 1953

7 Lee, C E *The Swansea and Mumbles Railway*, 1988

8 Oystermouth Rly Minutes, in Gittins, R, *Rock and Roll to Paradise*, 1982

9 *The Scotsman*, 9 November 1833

10 *Liverpool Mail*, 4 February 1860

11 G F Train's Obituary, *Lewiston Daily Sun* 23 January 1904

12 *The Age*, Melbourne 10 September 1858

13 *Liverpool Mercury* 3 February 1860

14 *Liverpool Daily Post* 3 July 1861

15 Horne and Maund, *Liverpool Transport Vol 1*, 1975

16 *Journal of the Society of Arts* 13 February 1857

17 W Bridges Adams, *Westminster Review*, as referred to in (14) above

18 Institution of Mechanical Engineers, *Proceedings* April 1880

19 *Lloyd's List*, as referred to in (6) above

20 J Nelson's letter of 5 January 1893 as referred to in (6) above

21 *The Railway News* 10 November 1877

22 Train, G F *Observations on Horse Railways ...*, 1860

23 *Caledonian Mercury*, 9 August 1860

24 *op. cit.* (23) page 47

25 Clark, D Kinnear *Op cit* (3) above

26 Train, G F *Observations on Horse Railways* 1860

27 *Birmingham Journal*, 4 August 1860

28 *Jackson's Oxford Journal*, 7 July 1860

29 Maund and Jenkins, *The Tramways of Birkenhead and Wallasey* 1987

30 *Liverpool Mercury*, 18 April 1860

31 *ibid*, 5 June 1860

32 *Liverpool Daily Post*, 8 August 1860

33 *ibid*, 12 July 1860

34 *ibid*, 21 August 1860

35 *Freeman's Journal*, 24 August 1860

36 *Liverpool Mercury*, 16 October 1867

37 *Chambers Dictionary*

38 *London Daily News*, 29 April 1861

39 *Liverpool Mercury*, 31 August 1860

40 *Liverpool Daily Post*, 31 August 1860

41 *Morning Chronicle*, 31 August 1860

42 Maund and Jenkins, *Op cit* (29) above

43 Price, J H *The Tram of 1860*, in *Modern Tramway*, August 1960

44 *Liverpool Daily Post*, 4 February 1861

45 Train, GF *Observations on Street Railways (Second Edition)* 1860

46 Lee and Nightingale, *Report of the Banquet ... 1860*, reprint by Adam Gordon 2004

47 *Liverpool Mercury*, 11 September 1860

48 *Scotsman*, 29 September 1860

49 *ibid*, 20 November 1860

50 *Scottish Press* [Edinburgh] 3 November 1860

51 *Glasgow Herald*, 1 September 1860

52 *Liverpool Mercury*, 20 November 1860

53 *Cheshire Observer*, 13 October 1860

54 *Morning Post*, 19 January 1861

55 *Liverpool Daily Post*, 8 May 1861

56 *ibid*, 10 July 1861

57 *Cheshire Observer*, 5 October 1861

58 *ibid*, 9 November 1861

59 *Liverpool Mercury*, 5 February 1862

60 *ibid*, 8 February 1862

61 *ibid*, 14 February 1862

62 *Cheshire Observer*, 15 March 1862

63 *Cheshire Observer*, 23 August & 27 September 1862

64 *ibid*, 5 March 1864

65 *London Standard*, 12 April 1869

66 *London City Press*, 27 October 1860

67 *London Daily News*, 7 September 1853

68 *ibid*, 12 February 1857

69 *London Standard*, 19 February 1858

70 *Morning Post*, 16 March 1858

71 *Morning Chronicle*, 15 March 1858

72 *London City Press*, 18 August 1860

73 Greene & Rippon, *Street Railways in London (Special Reports of Saint Marylebone …)* 1860

74 Rippon, GP *The application of G F Train of Boston to Establish Street Railways in London*, 1860

75 *South London Chronicle*, 15 September 1860

76 *Shoreditch Observer*, 22 September 1860

77 *London Daily News*, 8 October 1860

78 *Morning Chronicle*, 12 October 1860

79 *Lloyd's Weekly Newspaper*, 4 November 1860

80 *Shoreditch Observer*, 13 October 1860

81 *London Standard*, 18 October 1860

82 *Morning Post*, 29 September 1860

83 *ibid*, 24 October 1860

84 *London City Press*, 27 October 1860

85 *West Middlesex Advertiser*, 10 November 1860

86 *London City Press*, 15 December 1860

87 *East London Observer*, 29 December 1860

88 *Shoreditch Observer*, 16 February 1861

89 *American Engineer*, 8 December 1860, as quoted in (44) above

90 *Daily News.* and *Liverpool Mercury*, 25 December 1860

91 *Freeman's Journal*, Dublin 26 March 1860

92 *op. cit.* (27) above

93 *Morning Chronicle*, 19 March 1861

94 *Lloyd's Weekly Newspaper*, 7 April 1861

95 *Morning Chronicle*, 25 March 1861

96 *London Daily News*, 1 April 1861

97 *Kentish Chronicle*, 6 April 1861

98 *Hereford Journal*, 14 August 1861

99 *Morning Post*, 7 June 1861

100 *The Era*, 7 July 1861

101 *ibid*, 6 April 1861

102 *London Standard*, 16 April 1861

103 *Morning Post*, 21 May 1861

104 *Chassell's Illustrated Family Paper*, 11 May 1861

105 *The Lady's Newspaper*, 18 May 1861

106 *Freeman's Journal*, Dublin 26 March 1861

107 *Shoreditch Observer*, 22 September 1860

108 *The Engineer*, 28 September 1860

109 *Belfast Newsletter*, 11 October 1860

110 *Jackman's Oxford Journal*, 13 October 1860

111 *Aris's Birmingham Gazette*, 1 June 1861

112 *Birmingham Daily Post*, 5 June 1861

113 *ibid*, 23 September 1861

114 *Daily News*, 16 April 1861

115 *Morning Chronicle*, 25 November 1861

116 *The Argus* [Melbourne] 9 July 1861, quoting from the *Lincolnshire Times*, 16 April 1861

117 *Glasgow Herald*, 28 November 1860

118 Horne & Maund, *Liverpool Transport Volume One*, 1975

119 *Morning Chronicle*, 4 & 11 September 1860

120 *Jackman's Oxford Journal*, 6 April 1861

121 *Morning Chronicle*, 28 August 1861

122 *op cit* (20) above

123 *Freeman's Journal*, Dublin 29 June 1861

124 *Reynolds's News*, 30 June 1861

125 *Morning Chronicle,* 25 June 1861

126 *Daily News*, 26 June 1861

127 *Morning Chronicle*, 26 June 1861

128 *Political Examiner*, 29 June 1861

129 *Reynolds's Newspaper*, 14 July 1861

130 *London Daily News*, 21 June 1861

131 *ibid*, 6 July 1861

132 *Morning Chronicle*, 10 August 1861

133 *West Middlesex Advertiser*, 20 July 1861

134 *London Standard*, 16 August 1861

135 *Morning Chronicle*, 7 September 1861

136 *East London Observer*, 21 September 1861

137 *London Daily News*, 21 September 1861

138 *The Examiner*, 21 September 1861

139 *Shoreditch Observer*, 26 October 1861

140 *Morning Chronicle*, 10 December 1861

141 *ibid*, 11 February 1862

142 *ibid*, 29 March 1862

143 *South London Chronicle*, 4 January 1862

144 *East London Observer*, 12 April 1862

145 *London Daily News*, 21 June 1862

146 *Punch*, 4 January 1862

147 *Daily News*, 4 February 1862

148 Primatesta, A *Les Tramways Genevois*, 2005

149 Clark, D K, *Tramways, their construction and working*, London 1894

150 *Horse drawn trams of the Russian Empire* Skyscrapercity web forum

151 *Street Railway Journal*, 15 May 1892

152 *Birmingham Daily Post*, 12 December 1862

153 *Sheffield Telegraph*. 6 December 1871

154 *North Devon Journal*, 8 May 1862

155 Taplin, M R *Købenshavns Sporveje*, 1968; and *op cit* (28) above

156 Frohberg, U *Die Strassenbahn in Kopenhagen*, 1999

157 *Sporvogne i Danmark 1863–1972*

158 Walker, P J *One Hundred years of the Berlin Trams*, 1969

159 *The Times*, 10 January 1861

160 *Trolley Wire*, Ken McCarthy, December 1981

161 *Maitland Mercury*, 27 July 1861

162 *Empire*, 3 August 1861

163 *Sydney Morning Herald*, 21 August 1861

164 ibid, 21 December 1861

165 *Empire*, 31 August 1861

166 National Archives of Australia C4078, N7037

167 *Sydney Daily Mail*, 28 December 1861

168 *Empire*, 18 October 1862

169 *Sydney Morning Herald*, 21 January 1864

170 *Sydney Daily Mail*, 13 May 1864

171 Chinn, N & McCartney, K, *New South Wales Tramcar Handbook Part 2* 1976

172 op cit (1) page 270

173 *The Argus, Melbourne*, 17 June 1861

174 *The Star, Ballarat*, quoting from *The Argus*, 12 March 1862

175 *The Argus*, 30 August 1878

176 *Darlington Telegraph*, 7 December 1861

177 *ibid*, 28 December 1861

178 *ibid*, 4 January 1862

179 *Leeds Mercury*, 2 January 1862

180 *Darlington and Stockton Tines*, 4 January 1862

181 *ibid*, 16 July 1864

182 *ibid*, 5 November 1864

183 *ibid*, 6 August 1864

184 *ibid*, 3 September 1864

185 *ibid*, 24 December 1864

186 *Newcastle Journal*, 18 February 1864

187 *Darlington Telegraph*, 8 January 1865

188 *York Herald*, 11 November 1865

189 *Birmingham Daily Post*, 14 October 1861

190 *Staffordshire Sentinel*, 21 March 1863

191 *Birmingham Gazette*, 5 November 1864

192 *Birmingham Daily Post*, 14 November 1861

193 *ibid*, 20 November 1861

194 *ibid*, 1 February 1862

195 *ibid*, 22 March 1866

196 *ibid*, 3 February 1863

197 *Staffordshire Sentinel*, 12 September 1863

198 *ibid*, 17 October 1863

199 *Birmingham Daily Post*, 1 March 1864

200 *Proceedings of the Select Committee on Tramways Bill*, 4 April 1870

201 Bennet, EA *The Old Wives' Tale*, 1908

202 *John Bull*, 15 February 1862

203 *Dublin Evening Mail*, 3 October 1862

204 *Belfast Newsletter*, 11 November 1862

205 Thornton, W *The Nine Lives of Citizen Train*, New York, 1948

206 *The Times*, 6 March 1868

207 *Street Railway Review*, 15 September 1892

208 Thornton, W *The Nine Lives of Citizen Train*, New York, 1948

209 Train, GF *My Life in Many States and in Foreign Lands*, 1902

210 Foster, A *Around the World with Citizen Train*, 2002, from the *Phrenological Journal*, May 1904

211 *New York Times*, 1906

212 *Glasgow Herald*, 28 November 1860

213 *ibid*, 12 February 1862

214 *Darlington and Stockton Times*, 30 November 1861

215 *Liverpool Daily Post*, 1 December 1856

216 *ibid*, 18 September 1858

217 *Liverpool Daily Post*, 12 March 1860

218 *ibid*, 1 May 1860.

219 *op cit* (22 above)

220 *Liverpool Daily Post* advertisement, 22 March 1861

221 *Morning Post*, 19 July 1862

222 *ibid*, 5 December 1862

223 *Freeman's Journal*, 18 April 1863

224 *Gloucester Journal*, 21 July 1866

225 *Track and Trackless*, P R Coates, 1976

226 *Private communication*, P R Coates to J R Stevens, 1997

227 *130 jaar tram in Den Haag Pt 1*, van Donsetaar and Klamp, 1994

228 *London Daily News*, 13 March 1864

229 *ibid*, 2 April 1866

230 *Essex Standard*, 8 December 1865

231 *London Daily News*, 2 April 1866

232 *Perry's Bankrupt Gazette*, 29 December 1866

233 *Morning Post*, 11 June 1867

234 *Great Exhibition Catalogue* 1851, Class V, Item 530

235 *Morning Post*, 3 February and 22 April 1865

236 *London Standard*, 14 April 1865

237 *Pall Mall Gazette*, 15 December 1865

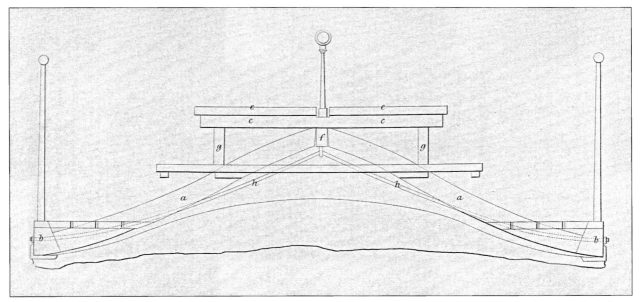

From *Liverpool Daily Post*, 22 March 1861

In October 1860 E F Prentiss patented this arrangement for top deck seat support, with the weight transferred to the sides of the car. This arrangement appears to have been incorporated in the design of his open carriage illustrated on page 77.

Index

Birkenhead Museum has this model of an early horse tram. Unfortunately nothing is known of its provenance. Although it appears to be a fairly accurate representation, several elements are quite crude. The authors (and the Museum) would be very glad to hear from any reader who can throw any light on its origins.